LEASE RENEWAL

LEASE RENEWAL

Camilla Lamont
Anne Seifert
Myriam Stacey

Acknowledgements

Crown copyright material is reproduced with the permission of the Controller of HMSO and the Queen's Printer for Scotland.

Please note: References to the masculine include, where appropriate, the feminine.

Published by RICS Business Services Limited
a wholly owned subsidiary of
The Royal Institution of Chartered Surveyors
under the RICS Books imprint
Surveyor Court
Westwood Business Park
Coventry CV4 8JE
UK

ISBN 1 84219 226 4

Typeset in Great Britain by Columns Design Ltd, Reading
Printed in Great Britain by Bell & Bain, Glasgow

Contents

Contents

Contents

Preface

While chartered surveyors may not need the *breadth* of understanding of the law of their opposite numbers in the legal profession, in a number of key areas of application to property and construction, they need a similar *depth* of legal knowledge. Exactly what the key areas may be depends to some extent on the nature of the surveyor's practice, but the law relating to landlord and tenant is an obvious example. There are plenty of chartered surveyors who would need to know more about the law relating to commercial leases (as well as valuation aspects) than the average lawyer in general practice.

So surveyors need law and, for a variety of reasons, need to maintain and develop their understanding of it. Changing trends or individual variations in clients' requirements mean that from time to time even the best practitioners (perhaps especially the best practitioners) will feel the need to expand their knowledge. The knowledge required at college or in studying for the Assessment of Professional Competence (APC) needs to be updated constantly to maintain its currency. Even specialists working in their areas of expertise need a source of reference as an aide-mémoire or as a first port of call in more detailed research.

The Case in Point series

RICS Books is committed to meeting the needs of surveyors (and other) professionals and the Case in Point series typifies that commitment. It is aimed at those who need to upgrade or update their legal knowledge, or those who need to have access to a good first reference at the outset of an inquiry. A particular difficulty is the burgeoning of reported decisions of the courts. The sheer scale of law reports, both general and specialist, makes it very hard even to be aware of recent trends, let alone identify the significance of an individual decision. The series seeks to address that difficulty by focussing on the body of case law and developments in it, in a defined area. In any given matter, the practitioner will want to be directed efficiently and painlessly to the decision which bears upon the matter he or she is dealing with, in other words to – the Case in Point.

The books in the Case in Point series offer a wealth of legal information which is essential in its practical application to the surveyor's work. Authors invited to write for the series have the level of expertise required to be selective and succinct, thus achieving a high degree of relevance without sacrificing accessibility. The series is developing incrementally and forms a collection of specialist books which can deliver what busy practitioners need – the law on the matter they are handling, when they want it.

Lease Renewal: Anne Seifert, Camilla Lamont and Myriam Stacey

Landlord and tenant work is at the heart of the practice of many chartered surveyors and this has been reflected in the commissioning of the Case in Point titles. *Lease Renewal*, with *Rent Review* and *Service Charges*, is intended to form part of the property core of the series. The basis of the subject is, of course, statutory and concerns the security of tenure regime for business tenants under the *Landlord and Tenant Act* 1954. Fifty years of the operation of this legislation were marked by the implementation on 1 June 2004 of the *Regulatory Reform (Business Tenancies) (England and Wales) Order* 2003 and a welcome summary of the main changes introduced can be found in chapter 1. However, if some foreign visitor, from a civil law system, imagined that the Act and its various amendments comprised the law on commercial lease renewals, they would be more than a little taken aback by the sheer scale of the case law: the authors refer to 60 cases on the questions as to whether the Act applies alone. Nor have the authors only accumulated the classic cases such as *Addiscombe Garden Estates v Crabbe* or *O'May v City of London Real Property* from past decades, although these are properly and necessarily represented; there are some 30 new cases since 2000 covered here, many deciding important points, such as *J Murphy & Sons v Railtrack* on the question of implied disregards for calculation of rent.

Two themes of this casebook are likely to be especially welcomed by practising chartered surveyors as reflecting the main areas of their professional activity. The first is procedure. The 1954 Act is notoriously heavy on steps to be taken and hoops to be gone through. While it would be asking too much to expect that the (frequent) judicial interventions are seen as positively helpful, practitioners would hardly wish to embark on service of section 25 and 26 notices without familiarity with the decisions in chapters 5–7; the courts have produced essential guidance.

The second main theme is that of dispute resolution, not merely in the procedure for making application to the court but in the practical processes of preparing and giving expert witness evidence (chapter 9). The sheer volume of cases is a reminder that commercial lease renewal is a highly contentious arena in which the stakes are often substantial. It is curiously fitting that the current combatants and their professional advisors can derive guidance in the resolution of their own disputes from the outcomes of previous contests.

RICS Books has been able to commission authors of considerable professional standing to tackle this exacting subject. All are barristers practising at Landmark Chambers in Bream's Buildings, off Chancery Lane, which is one of the leading property and development sets. Anne Seifert has over 20 years' experience at the property bar. A Fellow of the Chartered Institute of Arbitrators, she has chaired Rent Assessment Panels and regional Lands Tribunal hearings on a number of occasions. Camilla Lamont formerly taught property law at New College, Oxford University and has published and lectured widely in the field. She has a growing High Court and Leasehold Valuation Tribunal practice as an advocate. Myriam Stacey was called to the Bar in 1998 and has already established a good practice in landlord and tenant law, including appearance in reported cases.

Together, the authors have been able to deal successfully with a challenging task and have produced a vital addition to the Case in Point series.

Anthony Lavers, 2005.
Professional Support Lawyer, White & Case, London.
Visiting Professor of Law, Oxford Brookes University, Oxford.
Consultant Editor, Case in Point Series.

List of Acts, Statutory Instruments and abbreviations

The following Acts and Statutory Instruments are referenced in this publication. Where an Act or Statutory Instrument is mentioned frequently, it is referred to by the abbreviation in brackets that follows.

Agricultural Holdings Act 1948
Agricultural Holdings Act 1986
Cost of Leases Act 1958
Human Rights Act 1998
Industrial and Provident Societies Act 1893
Landlord and Tenant Act 1927 (**'1927 Act'**)
Landlord and Tenant Act 1954 (**'1954 Act'**)
Landlord and Tenant (Covenants) Act 1995 (**'1995 Act'**)
Landlord and Tenant (Licensed Premises) Act 1990
Law of Property Act 1925
Law of Property Act 1969
Law of Property (Miscellaneous Provisions) Act 1989
Recorded Delivery Service Act 1962
Rent Act 1957
Rent Act 1968
Rent Act 1977
Town and Country Planning Act 1971
Town and Country Planning Act 1990

Civil Procedure Rules 1998 (SI 1998/3132) (**'CPR'**)
Counter-Inflation (Business Rents) Order 1972 (SI 1972/1850)
Landlord and Tenant Act 1954, Part II (Notices) Regulations 1983 (SI 1983/133)
Landlord and Tenant Act 1954, Part 2 (Notices) Regulations 2004 (SI 2004/1005)

Landlord and Tenant Act (Appropriate Multiplier) Order 1990 (SI 1990/363)

Regulatory Reform (Business Tenancies) (England and Wales) Order 2003 (SI 2003/3096) (**'2003 Order'**)

The text of this publication is divided into commentary and case summaries. The commentary is enclosed between grey highlighted lines for ease of reference.

Table of Cases

1
Introduction

1.1 SECURITY OF TENURE FOR BUSINESS TENANTS

This book deals with the statutory scheme of security of tenure conferred on tenants of business premises in England and Wales by Part II of the *Landlord and Tenant Act* 1954 ('1954 Act') and the cases that have been decided under that legislation. The aim is to guide the reader through the process of a business lease renewal.

Landlord and Tenant Act 1954, Part II

The basic effect of the 1954 Act can be summarised as follows:

- Tenants of business premises have a general right to renew their leases. On the termination of the existing contractual tenancy a statutory continuation tenancy arises which can only be terminated in accordance with the provisions of the Act by the service of a section 25 notice (by the landlord) or the making of a section 26 request (by the tenant). The tenant then has the right to apply to court for the grant of a new tenancy. Chapters 2, 4 to 6 and 12 herein deal with the issues of when the Act applies and the mechanics of the lease renewal process.
- The parties can contract out of the security for tenure provisions provided certain formalities are complied with. The contracting out provisions are covered by Chapter 3.
- Landlords can oppose the grant of a new lease on certain specified grounds. The grounds of opposition are covered in Chapter 6.
- Tenants may in some circumstances be entitled to compensation for having to leave the premises, most notably where the landlord successfully opposes the grant of a new lease on the grounds that it intends to redevelop. The compensation provisions are considered in Chapter 10.
- The rent under the new tenancy is the open market rent. The new lease cannot be for a term exceeding 15 years and will

generally be on the same terms as the previous tenancy. Disputes as to the terms of the new tenancy are discussed in Chapter 8.

This remains the general picture under the Act today, despite the various amendments introduced over the years by the *Law of Property Act* 1969, the *Landlord and Tenant (Licensed Premises) Act* 1990 and, most recently, the *Regulatory Reform (Business Tenancies) (England and Wales) Order* 2003 ('2003 Order').

1.2 RECENT REFORMS

Regulatory Reform (Business Tenancies) (England and Wales) Order 2003

The most recent reforms (brought into force on 1 June 2004) have been largely improvements of detail rather than changes of principle (see summary of main changes below). The reforms introduced by the 2003 Order amend the provisions of the 1954 Act itself. This book has been written taking into account the changes to the Act made by the 2003 Order. However, the old rules will continue to apply to some renewals and reference should be made to the transitional provisions.

1.2.1 Main changes introduced on 1 June 2004

The main changes introduced by the 2003 Order include:

- introducing new safeguards for tenants agreeing to exclude security of tenure (contracting out), while removing the need to obtain court permission;
- clarifying what a tenant must do to terminate a tenancy in the section 25 notice;
- abolishing the requirement for a tenant to serve a counter-notice;
- allowing either party to apply to the court for renewal of the tenancy and introducing new time limits for applications and enabling the parties to agree to extend these;
- permitting the tenant, as well as the landlord, to apply for an interim rent;

- making it obligatory to respond accurately to a section 40 notice for information; and
- amending the length of lease the court can now order to 15 years rather than just a 14-year term.

1.2.2 **Transitional provisions**

The 2003 Order does not affect:

- any notice or request served under sections 25 and/or 26 prior to 1 June 2004 or anything done in consequence of such a notice or request;
- any notice served under section 27(2) given by the tenant to his immediate landlord prior to 1 June 2004; or
- an agreement to surrender, or exclusion of sections 24 to 28 by the court, made or authorised prior to 1 June 2004.

As the lease renewal process is initiated either by the service of a section 25 notice by the landlord seeking to terminate the tenancy or by the tenant making a section 26 request for a new tenancy, it will be important to consider whether the relevant notice or request was given and/or made prior to 1 June 2004.

If the relevant notice was served prior to 1 June 2004, the old regime applies to that notice and to all ensuing procedures.

However, if the relevant notice was served on or after 1 June 2004, the new regime will govern the notice and everything else done in consequence of it. This book is written on the basis that the new regime applies.

2
When the act applies

2.1   LANDLORD AND TENANT ACT 1954, SECTION 23

Section 23 provides that a tenancy is within the *Landlord and Tenant Act* 1954 ('1954 Act') if the whole or a part of the demised premises are occupied by the tenant for the purposes of his business or for those and other purposes. The expression 'business' includes any trade, profession or employment. It also includes any activity carried on by a body of persons, whether corporate or unincorporated. Therefore, there are three essential conditions for protection:

- There must be a tenancy – a mere licence does not confer statutory protection.
- The tenant must occupy at least part of the premises.
- The occupation by the tenant must be wholly or partly for business purposes. If there is only partial occupation by the tenant, or partial business use, the whole of the demised premises qualify for protection, although the tenant can only insist on a new tenancy of the part which he occupies.

By section 32(1), the tenant is entitled to a new tenancy of 'the holding' only.

The main importance of the holding is that it is only for the part of the demised premises which is within the definition of the holding that the tenant is entitled to a new tenancy. The premises are excluded from the holding when not occupied by the tenant or his employees.

2.2   ONLY TENANTS ARE PROTECTED

2.2.1 General principle

The 1954 Act applies to tenancies. It does not apply to licences to occupy premises.

Shell-Mex and BP Ltd v Manchester Garages Ltd (1971)

An agreement for the occupation of a petrol filling station was held to be a licence rather than a tenancy. Lord Justice Buckley said:

> 'One has to find out what is the true nature of the transaction and then see how the Act operates upon that state of affairs, if it bites at all. One should not approach the problem with a tendency to attempt to find a tenancy because unless there is a tenancy the case will escape the effect of the statute.'

Bruton v London and Quadrant Housing Trust (1999)

The House of Lords held that the extent of possession depends on the intention of the parties, objectively ascertained by reference to the language of the agreement and relevant background. In this case, it was found that the agreement gave the appellant exclusive possession.

London & Associated Investment Trust plc v Calow & another (1986)

The principles laid down by Lord Templeman in *Street v Mountford* (1985) applied to business tenancies. In *Street v Mountford*, which concerned residential premises, it was held that the grant of exclusive possession for a fixed or periodic term in consideration of a rent would result in the grant of a tenancy unless there are circumstances of legal significance to negative such a rent.

Dellneed Ltd & another v Chin (1986)

A management agreement was designed to reflect a traditional Chinese agreement known as a Mai Toi agreement. Under a Mai Toi agreement, an established restaurant owner allows a newcomer to the restaurant business who lacks capital and experience to use a fully equipped restaurant and trade on his own account bearing profits and losses in return for the payment of a weekly fee to the owner. It was held that the management agreement granted exclusive use of the premises. The effect of the transaction was to confer exclusive possession for a term at a rent and consequently created a tenancy.

National Car Parks Ltd v Trinity Development Co (Banbury) Ltd (2001)

The claimant agreed to pay a specified percentage of profits for the right to operate a shopper's car park. It was held that the agreement was a licence. It was for a term and at a rent, but it did not grant to the claimant a right to keep out the person who had granted it. The agreement did not grant exclusive possession.

Smith & another v Northside Developments Ltd & another (1987)

A and B carried on business in different parts of shop space in part of the ground floor of a building. After a time B left and A occupied the whole of the shop space, paying double the previous weekly amount. There was no agreement in writing. A claimed it had not merely taken over the space from B, but had obtained an exclusive right of occupation. It was held that there was no evidence of an agreement granting exclusive possession, there was merely an arrangement to have no replacement for the person who had vacated.

Dresden Estates Ltd v Collinson (1987)

An agreement was called a licence and stated that exclusive possession of a workshop and store had not been granted. It also contained some provisions found in tenancies. It was held that the agreement created a licence. In particular, a provision by which the occupier could be moved from time to time to other premises in the owner's adjoining property was inconsistent with a right to exclusive possession and was inconsistent with a tenancy. The decision was based on the particular facts and the agreement in question.

Essex Plan Ltd v Broadminster Ltd (1988)

An agreement granted the plaintiffs the right to occupy the premises for the purposes of their market in which they would allow stall holders to operate, and provided for the licence fees, payment of rates and other outgoings. The agreement was for a year with an option to take a lease for 30 years, which was not exercised. The plaintiffs claimed the agreement created a tenancy. It was held that exclusive possession was not conferred and the agreement created a licence and not a tenancy.

Esso Petroleum Co, Ltd v Fumegrange and others (1994)

There were three agreements in respect of a petrol filling station. The first was a partnership agreement called a licence. The second was a shop franchise agreement that required F to operate an 'Esso Shop' in accordance with the provisions of a manual. The third was an agreement for the operation of a car wash. It was held that the agreements gave E the right to possession, the right to make alterations, the right to install a car wash and to change the layout of the shop. The rights of E had to be looked at cumulatively and were inconsistent with an exclusive right of possession having been given to F. The agreements had not created a tenancy.

Cardiothoracic Institute v Shrewdcrest Ltd (1986)

Three successive tenancies of business premises had been granted following the joint applications of the landlord and tenant to court for orders to exclude the protection of the 1954 Act. Before the end of the third tenancy, negotiations began for a further application to court and a further short term tenancy. Several short extensions were agreed. The tenant remained in occupation paying rent.

The tenant then claimed it was entitled to a periodic tenancy protected by Part II of the 1954 Act. It was held that the tenancy was not protected.

- Each extension was negotiated subject to a condition that the extension should be the subject of a tenancy agreement approved by the County Court excluding the operation of sections 24 to 28 of the Act.
- It was intended by both parties that there would be no binding tenancy agreement between them until approval of the County Court was obtained.
- The payment and acceptance of rent, during the holding over pending a new tenancy, did not create a periodic tenancy in this case.

Wroe v Exmos Cover Ltd (2000)

'A licence for the use of Business Premises' was granted by E to W. The agreement expired. A director of E wrote a letter to W stating that he accepted that W was a tenant. A section 25 notice was served opposing a new tenancy on the ground of redevelopment. W served a counter notice and applied for a new tenancy. It was then contended that W had a licence not a tenancy. The question was whether a tenancy had been created by estoppel.

The Court of Appeal held that there was no tenancy by estoppel.

- The letter could not have created a tenancy by estoppel. It is a tenancy that creates an estoppel, not an estoppel that creates a tenancy.
- The landlord can agree to treat the tenant as having the same protection as if the tenancy fell within the 1954 Act and there is no reason why the tenant should not be able to rely on an estoppel to the same effect.
- However, in this case there was insufficient evidence of detrimental reliance to support an estoppel.

2.2.2 Tenancies at will

Tenancies at will, whether created expressly or by implication, are not within the protection of the 1954 Act. The reason is that the statutory machinery was not intended to operate on such tenancies.

Wheeler v Mercer (1956)

The House of Lords held that the 1954 Act did not apply to tenancies at will which arose by operation of law.

Manfield & Sons Ltd v Botchin (1970)

The landlord of business premises let a shop on a written tenancy at will until such time as it succeeded in getting permission to develop the site. After several years the landlord succeeded in obtaining permission to develop the site.

In an action for possession, the tenant claimed the protection of Part II of the 1954 Act. It was held by Cooke J that a tenancy at will created by express agreement did not fall within the scope of Part II of the 1954 Act. The landlord was entitled to possession.

Hagee (London) Ltd v AB Erikson and Larson (1975)

It was held in this case that Part II of the 1954 Act does not apply to a tenancy at will of business premises created by express agreement between the parties. It was stressed that the court will look very carefully at an agreement to see whether it is a genuine tenancy at will.

Javad v Aqil (1991)

It was held that the tenancy in this case was a tenancy at will.

- A tenancy at will springs from a consensual arrangement between the parties and the extent of the rights created depends of the intention of the parties.
- Where a prospective tenant is let into occupation in anticipation of terms being agreed, the fact that the parties have not yet agreed terms will be a relevant factor in ascertaining their intention.
- There may be an explanation of a payment of rent other than the creation of a periodic tenancy.

2.3   **APPLICATION TO SUBTENANTS**

Part II of the Landlord and Tenant Act 1954 Act applies to subtenants

Section 69 of the 1954 Act provides that 'tenancy' includes a tenancy created either immediately or derivatively out of the freehold, whether by lease or underlease, by an agreement for a lease or underlease or by a tenancy agreement.

2.3.1 **An unlawful subtenancy is within the statutory protection**

The following decision creates difficulties for landlords.

D'Silva v Lister House Development Ltd (1970)

A was the tenant of premises and B was the landlord under a lease that contained a covenant by A not to carry on any profession, trade or business in the property without prior consent of B. C, a doctor, entered into negotiations with A for a tenancy of a suite of rooms in the premises. A allowed C into possession to carry out redecoration on payment of a quarter's rent. B refused to grant a licence in respect of C's use of the premises.

It was held that:

■ C was entitled to protection under Part II of the 1954 Act as a subtenant; or
■ alternatively, C became a quarterly tenant of A by going into possession on payment of a quarter's rent and was equally entitled to the protection of Part II of the Act.

In the above case, section 23(4) of the 1954 Act (tenancy must not prohibit business use) was not applicable since C was not a party to the head lease (see 2.7.1 below).

2.4 **TENANCY MUST INCLUDE PREMISES CAPABLE OF BEING OCCUPIED**

2.4.1 **Meaning of 'premises'**

Bracy v Reed (1962)

The court found the defendant was a tenant and not a licensee of gallops.

The word 'premises' is not defined in the 1954 Act. It was held that 'premises' can be used in a strict legal and also in a popular sense. In this case, it was concluded that gallops were within the meaning of 'premises' within section 23(1) of the Act and that the tenancy was within the protection of the Act.

2.4.2 Rights of way

A tenancy of a right of way or similar right is not within the protection of Part II of the 1954 Act.

It may well be that a lease of premises together with a right of way is wholly within the protection of the Act.

Land Reclamation Co Ltd v Basildon District Council (1979)

A roadway owned by B was the only means of access to L's land that was used for waste disposal. L had a right of way over the roadway granted by a lease. It was held that Part II of the 1954 Act did not apply to the right of way.

- A tenant does not occupy a right of way as the word 'occupy' is normally understood.
- 'Premises' is not an appropriate word to describe an easement (right of way) standing by itself.

Whitley v Stumbles (1930)

The House of Lords held that Part I of the *Landlord and Tenant Act* 1927 extended to the whole of the subject matter of a lease of a hotel and fishing rights.

Nevill Long & Co (Boards) Ltd v Firmenich & Co (1983)

It was held that the 1954 Act applied in this case where a right of way over adjoining property of the landlord was included in a lease of business premises.

2.5 PREMISES MUST BE OCCUPIED BY THE TENANT

2.5.1 General principle

The general principle is that the tenant must occupy at least part of the premises.

2.5.2 **Are the premises occupied?**

Sometimes the question will be whether the property is occupied at all.

Wandsworth London Borough Council v Singh (1991)

Land had been leased to Wandsworth Council by the GLC in 1977. Dr Singh purchased the GLC's reversion. He wanted to obtain possession of the land to develop it commercially. The land measured about 75 ft by 75 ft and had been used for at least 13 years by local inhabitants for leisure and recreation. The site had a hard surface but there were trees and borders planted with shrubs and roses. It was partly enclosed by a wall with gates, which were locked from time to time. Visits by maintenance staff and subcontractors were at least once a week in summer and once a fortnight in winter. Notice was given and Wandsworth Council applied for a new tenancy.

The Court of Appeal held that Wandsworth Council were physically present and exercised control over the land by their servants or agents – if an ordinary man were asked, 'Who is in occupation of that open space?' he would answer, 'The Council is'.

2.5.3 **Who occupies the premises?**

There may be competition for the role of occupier. This is because commonly there is more than one person exercising or entitled to exercise rights over the same premises.

In such cases, a further test has to be applied to decide which of the persons is the occupier.

Lee-Verhulst (Investments) Ltd v Harwood Trust (1972)

A house had been subdivided into 20 fully furnished apartments. The tenant carried on the business of letting the apartments. He had the right of access to all parts of the property to provide services. The Court of Appeal held that the tenant occupied the whole of the property for the purpose of his business, even though each resident had exclusive occupation of his apartment as a residence for the purposes of the *Rent Act* 1968. The time and attention taken in running the business, the services rendered to the occupants and the degree of control exercised, were all relevant elements to be taken into account.

William Boyer & Sons v Adams (1975)

A was a tenant of a former farmhouse and outbuildings. He lived in the farmhouse and sublet the outbuildings for use as light industrial units. It was held that A was entitled to the protection of Part II of the 1954 Act in respect of the whole of the premises including the sublet units. A was acting not so much as a landlord passively receiving rent, but as a manager of a business activity earning profits by providing accommodation, facilities and services.

2.5.4 Employee accommodation

If a person takes a tenancy of residential premises for the purpose of providing accommodation for his employees, he may occupy the premises through his employees. The occupation will only be for the purposes of his business if it is necessary, and not merely convenient, for the employees to live at the premises in order to perform their duties properly.

Chapman v Freeman (1978)

The tenant of a cottage used it to provide accommodation for staff employed at his nearby hotel. The tenant claimed that the tenancy was subject to Part II of the 1954 Act as the cottage was occupied for the purposes of his hotel business within the meaning of section 23(1) of the Act. The Court of Appeal held that to be 'occupied for the purposes of a business' within the meaning of section 23(1) of the Act, premises had to be occupied for a purpose necessary to the furtherance of the business and not merely for the convenience of the business.

Groveside Properties v Westminster Medical School (1983)

It was held that a medical school occupied a flat used for medical students as study bedrooms. The occupation was evidenced by the substantial degree of control that it exercised and the furniture and equipment provided. The occupation was not simply for convenience. It was to achieve an educational purpose for the advancement of the students' medical training.

Linden v Department of Health and Social Security (1986)

A house was let to the Secretary of State for Social Services and converted by him into eight self-contained residential flats to provide accommodation for hospital employees. The district health authority managed the flats on his behalf. Employees of the health service resided in the flats. The flats were fully furnished and equipped with cutlery, crockery and blankets, but with no bed linen. They were occupied rent free but with agreed salary deduction from the occupants. It was held that the degree of management was such that the district health authority was in occupation.

Hancock & Willis v GMS Syndicate Ltd (1983)

A firm of solicitors had unlimited rights to use a small part of a building that they had allowed a printing company to use as its offices. The question was whether the solicitors remained in occupation. It was held that the phrase 'occupied for the purposes of a business carried on by him' in section 23 of the 1954 Act imported an element of control and use and involved the notion of physical control.

2.5.5 The 'thread of continuity' must not be broken

There need not be continuous day-to-day trading for there to be occupation for business purposes within section 23 of the 1954 Act provided the 'thread of continuity' is not broken.

Where 'the thread of continuity' had not been broken

I & H Caplan Ltd v Caplan (No 2) (1963)

The tenants were in occupation of the premises for the purposes of their retail business at the time when they made an application for a new tenancy and for some time afterwards. It was held on the hearing of a preliminary issue that the landlord had proved a ground of opposition to the new tenancy. The tenants appealed against the order and they went out of occupation. Within a year, the appeal came before the Court of Appeal and was allowed, the effect of which was that the landlord's ground of opposition was not established. The tenants went back into occupation. The landlords claimed that the thread of continuity had been broken. It was held that the thread of continuity had not been broken. A tenant does not lose protection of the 1954 Act simply by ceasing to occupy the premises.

Morrison Holdings Ltd v Manders Property (Wolverhampton) Ltd (1976)

The reason why the tenant was not trading at the material time was because the premises had been severely damaged by fire. There was no suggestion that the tenant, through his own fault, had caused the fire. The Court of Appeal held that in the circumstances the thread of continuity had not been broken.

Where the 'thread of continuity' had been broken

Aspinall Finance Ltd v Viscount Chelsea (1989)

The tenant, A, applied for a new tenancy of premises which had been used as a gaming club. The premises ceased to be physically occupied in 1984 because the Aspinall group of which A was a part, wished to run a gaming club in a more attractive building in a different area of London. To do this it required a gaming licence, which could only be obtained by the surrender of the licence covering the premises. However, it was their intention to reopen the premises as a gaming club as soon as a new lease under the 1954 Act and a fresh licence could be obtained. A applied for a new lease in 1986.

It was held that the 'thread of continuity' had been broken. In 1984 the tenants had a clear commercial choice. They exercised it, ceased to carry on business, and had not carried it on since. The intention to reopen was not enough.

2.5.6 Seasonal businesses

Teasdale v Walker (1958)

The premises in this case were near the front of a seaside resort and were used for 'mock auctions'. They were open only at Easter, Whitsun and from July to the end of September. The Court of Appeal held that the 'thread of continuity' had been broken in this case. It is a question of fact and degree whether the premises used for summer purposes are so occupied during the winter months. The answer to the question will depend partly on the length of the gap between the intermittent activities.

Artemiou v Procopiou (1965)

This case concerned a café and restaurant business. Lord Justice Salmon said:

> 'It seems clear to me that anyone who goes into occupation of premises in which a seasonal business is carried on is occupying them all year round for the purposes of the business; if not, it is difficult to see for what other purpose he would be occupying them during the out-of-season months.'

2.5.7 Special cases

There are special rules in the 1954 Act for dealing with situations where the occupying business is not carried on by the tenant but:

- by a partnership of which the tenant is a member (see section 41A);
- by a limited company where the tenant has a controlling interest in the company carrying on the business from the premises (or vice versa) (sections 23 and 46);

- by a member of a group of companies (section 42);
- where there is a trust relationship between the persons carrying on the business and the tenant (section 41).

There are also special rules concerning occupation by government departments.

Partnerships: section 41A

Section 41A provides that the actions under the 1954 Act which would normally require the concerted conduct of all the tenants can be effected by those of the tenants whom carry on the business without the other tenants (i.e. where some of the tenants are active in the business and some are not).

Limited companies: section 23(1A) and 23(1B)

Prior to the *Regulatory Reform (Business Tenancies) (England and Wales) Order* 2003, a tenancy would be unprotected by the 1954 Act if the business in occupation was a limited company, but the tenant was a private individual, even if he was the sole shareholder and director. Section 23 of the 1954 Act now applies in this situation, and to the reverse case of a company being the tenant, provided that the individual has a 'controlling interest' in the company.

Group of companies: section 42

Provisions similar in principle apply as between companies within the same group. Companies that are a parent or subsidiary of each other or are both subsidiaries of another company are taken to be within the same group. Section 42 of the 1954 Act applies when the tenant's or landlord's interest is held by one company within a group of companies. Companies are within the same group when one is a subsidiary of the other or both are subsidiaries of a third company. 'Subsidiary' is defined as in the *Companies Act* 1985.

Trusts: section 41(1)

Section 41 provides that where the tenancy is held on trust, occupation and the carrying on of a business by any of the beneficiaries under the trust, is treated as equivalent to occupation and carrying on business by the tenant for the purposes of ascertaining whether the tenancy is within the protection of the Act.

2.6 TENANT'S OCCUPATION MUST BE (AT LEAST IN PART) FOR ITS BUSINESS PURPOSES

2.6.1 Definition of 'business'

The definition of 'business' in section 23(2) of the 1954 Act is widely drawn and includes a trade, profession or employment and any activity carried on by a body of persons, whether corporate or unincorporated.

Town Investments Ltd v Department of the Environment (1997)

In this case, the Crown's occupation of premises was held to be for the purposes of 'a business' carried on by the Crown as the tenant, within the definition of 'business tenancy' in article 2(2) of the *Counter-Inflation (Business Rents) Order* 1972. Lord Diplock described the word 'business' as an etymological chameleon; it suits its meaning to the context in which it is found.

Where the tenants are individuals rather than bodies of persons, the business must be a trade, profession or employment.

Lewis v Weldcrest Ltd (1978)

The applicant was the tenant of a house. She occupied one room and shared the kitchen, bathroom and one other room with her five lodgers, who occupied the three remaining rooms. She paid for the gas and electricity and provided some food. The Court of Appeal held that although the applicant's only gainful occupation was the taking in of lodgers, in view of the degree of that activity and the lack of commercial advantage, it could not be regarded as an occupation within the description of a 'trade, profession or employment' in section 23(2) of the 1954 Act. Therefore, since the 1954 Act could not apply, the applicant was a protected tenant under the *Rent Act* 1977.

Hillil Property and Investment Co Ltd v Naraine Pharmacy (1979)

A pharmacy business was carried on in two adjoining shops – numbers 25 and 27. The first and second defendants wanted to join 25 and 27 together structurally. They took an assignment of a nearby shop, number 33, in order to store building materials during the works with the intention of using it for business purposes once the works were complete. There was a substantial delay in the reconstruction works. The contractors used 33 to dump waste material taken from 25 and 27 and that was its use when the lease expired. The question was whether 33 was being used for the purposes of a business. The Court of Appeal held that an 'activity' for the purposes of section 23(2) of the 1954 Act, although it might be something that was not strictly a 'trade, profession or employment' must nevertheless be something that was correlative to the conceptions involved in those words. As a matter of fact and degree, the dumping of the spoil was not an 'activity' within the meaning of that phrase in section 23(2).

Groveside Properties Ltd v Westminster Medical School (1983)

The running of a major medical school is an 'activity'.

Secretary of State for Transport v Jenkins (2000)

The question in this case was whether the use of land as a 'community free farm' by the tenants was a 'business' within the meaning in section 23(2) of the 1954 Act. The community farm was a free farm. Visitors to it were not charged. The tenants had no intention to carry on a commercial enterprise. It was an enterprise not carried on with a view to profit. It was not carried on as a trading activity, but rather in a spirit of benevolence. It was held not to be a trade, profession or employment or any kind of business.

An inability to distribute profit does not prevent an operation from being a business.

Hawkesbrook Leisure Ltd v Reece-Jones Partnership (2003)

The claimant was a company formed to take leases and to manage two sports grounds owned by London Transport. It was a non-profit-making company limited by guarantee. It had its own ground staff managed bar and catering facilities at the sports grounds. It charged fees to London Transport, clubs and members of the public (who had to be members of the sports club) for the use of the grounds.

It was held that the claimant was in occupation for the purposes of section 23 of the 1954 Act. It was carrying on a commercial enterprise with a view to making a surplus, and aimed to make an accounting profit. It was irrelevant that its surplus could not be distributed to its shareholders or members. In any event, its business was an 'activity carried on by a body of persons' within the meaning of section 23.

Narcissi v Wolfe (1960)

The tenant occupied the ground and basement floors of premises for restaurant business purposes. The second and third floors were sublet for residential purposes. The first floor contained articles of furniture and the tenant used it for sleeping one night. The basement had been condemned as mostly unsuitable for the preparation and storage of food. The tenant wanted a contribution from the landlord towards the cost of renovation of the basement. It was held that although the occupation of the first floor by the tenant was for the purposes of assisting his obtaining a new lease, he was genuinely in need of storage accommodation for food. It was held that he was in occupation of the first floor for the purposes of section 23(1) of the 1954 Act.

Hills (Patents) Ltd v University College Hospital Board of Governors (1955)

The activities of governors of a hospital in administering the premises had been held to be a business.

Addiscombe Garden Estates Ltd v Crabbe (1957)

The trustees of a members' lawn tennis club registered under the *Industrial and Provident Societies Act* 1893 entered into an agreement with the owners of tennis courts and a clubhouse to use and enjoy the premises for two years in consideration of monthly payments of 'court fees'. It was held that the agreement created a tenancy and that the premises were occupied for the purposes of a 'business' as defined by section 23(2) of the 1954 Act, as the 'activity' of a lawn tennis club was carried on.

2.6.2 Purpose of occupation

A tenant occupies premises for the purposes of a business carried on by him only when the business activity is a significant purpose of his occupation of the premises.

Cheryl Investments Ltd v Saldanha; Royal Life Saving Society v Page (1978)

A doctor took a tenancy of a maisonette near his consulting rooms and as well as using it as his home saw a patient there very occasionally in an emergency, the tenancy was held not to be within the 1954 Act.

Gurton v Parrott and another (1991)

This case involved two factual situations.

In the first case, the letting was of a residential flat. The tenant was a partner in a business that the partners carried on from their respective homes. The tenant installed a telephone in the flat and placed office equipment in the entrance hall. Notepaper headed with the name of the business gave the telephone number of the flat. The tenant issued statements on the notepaper of the flat and had frequent visitors carrying briefcases. The Court of Appeal held that although the tenant occupied the flat as a dwelling as well as for the purposes of his business, the occupation for the purposes of his business was the significant purpose of

21

the occupation. He occupied the premises for the purposes of his business within section 23(1) of the 1954 Act.

In the second case, the tenant of a lease of a maisonette was a medical practitioner who had consulting rooms in nearby premises. He occupied the maisonette as his home but entered the address of both the consulting rooms and the maisonette in the medical directory and printed telephone numbers for both addresses on the separate notepaper at each address. The only professional use he made of the maisonette was to see a patient there once or twice a year in an emergency. The Court of Appeal held that the significant purpose for which the tenant occupied the maisonette was residential and it was not a business tenancy within section 23(1).

A sporadic spare-time activity may not amount to a business.

Abernethie v Kleiman Ltd (1969)

The tenant carried on a greengrocer's business in a shop and lived in rooms above. The tenancy also included a loft. He regularly taught scripture on Sundays to about 30 children for about an hour in the loft. He received no payment, but there was a subscription box into which donations could be made for a scripture mission. After a time he closed the shop owing to a decline in trade and from then on he held his scripture lessons on Sundays in the shop in summer and in his private sitting-room in winter. The landlords knew that he carried on a Sunday school and raised no objection. The Court of Appeal held that the pursuit by a person gratuitously of a spare time activity in his own home was not a 'trade, profession or employment' within section 23 of the 1954 Act and therefore the tenant was not carrying on a 'business' within the meaning of the Act.

Harley Queen v Forsyte Kerman (1983)

It was held in the County Court that a quarterly tenancy of a numbered parking bay in a basement garage of a block of flats used by a firm of solicitors to park a partner's car was a business tenancy.

Simmonds v Egyed (1985)

The County Court held that there was no business tenancy where the tenant was a self-employed decorator who had notepaper printed with his home address and telephone number, on which it was stated that he was a decorator. His wife typed his estimates and bills at home and kept the books, but he kept his decorating equipment elsewhere. In his business accounts, he claimed a proportion of the rent and telephone bill against tax.

The activity of subletting may be a business but its nature will often mean that the tenant does not occupy the premises personally and the occupation requirement will not be satisfied.

Bagettes Ltd v GP Estates Ltd (1956)

There was a lease of premises containing 13 residential flats. The lease expired. By that time three of the 13 flats were already or became vacant. The tenants under the lease claimed a new tenancy of the premises under Part II of the 1954 Act. The Court of Appeal held that the tenancy was not a business tenancy. The tenants used the entire premises for the purposes of a business carried on by them (i.e. subletting the premises in flats). However, the tenants were not entitled to a new tenancy because:

(1) the holding excluded the flats sublet (as they were not in the tenants' occupation); and
(2) if those flats were left out of consideration, no business purpose remained for which the tenants could maintain that they were occupying the holding, that is to say, the rest of the premises.

Ross Auto Wash Ltd v Herbert and another (1978)

This case concerned premises in which a variety of licensees holding concessions sold articles from stands. The tenant's business was the granting of licences to the concession holders. The question was whether the tenant, or another company, both controlled by the same individual, actually carried on the business. It was held that the tenant carried on the business and that it occupied the premises for that purpose.

Trans-Brittania Properties Ltd v Darby Properties Ltd (1986)

Premises were used by the tenants for the carrying on of the business of lock-up garages. The majority of the garages were sublet, some were vacant and one garage was used by the tenants as a store room. The tenants, although not under contractual obligation to do so, carried out some maintenance and cleaning and sometimes with the consent of the subtenant, would make some internal repairs to a garage. There was no office or living accommodation on the site, no water, no electricity, no security guard, and regular visits by the tenant's staff were only fortnightly. The Court of Appeal held that the occupation requirement in section 23 of the 1954 Act was not satisfied.

Graysim Holdings Ltd v P & O Property Holdings Ltd (1996)

Where a tenant of business premises who sublets part of the property to a business subtenant on terms which would have the legal result that thereafter the sublet property would form the holding of the subtenant's business tenancy, the part sublet cannot remain part of the holding of the tenant's business tenancy.

Bassari Ltd v Camden London Borough (1999)

B was the tenant of a property comprising a basement, a ground floor shop and four upper floors containing flats. The flats were occupied by individual residents apart from one that was retained by the B for storage. B was supposed to provide services such as supply of toiletries together with a cleaning service and an answering service for the telephone, dry cleaning, a laundry service, television, tea and coffee, and continental breakfast. There was no evidence that such services were in fact provided. B claimed to be in business occupation of the flats. It was held that there was insufficient retention of control to justify a finding that B was in occupation of the flats.

However, the tenant may retain sufficient control over the units sublet or occupied under licence to be in occupation itself for the purposes of a business it runs. The occupation requirement was satisfied in *Lee-Verhulst (Investments) Ltd v Harwood Trust* (1972) and *William Boyer & Sons Ltd v Adams* (1975). (See 2.5.3 above.)

2.7 TENANCY MUST NOT PROHIBIT BUSINESS USE

The principles underlying section 23(4) of the 1954 Act may be summarised as follows:

- A business use in breach of a covenant prohibiting business use extending to the whole of the premises means that the tenancy is not within the Act. The tenancy is within the Act if the covenant extends only to a part of the demised premises.
- A business use in breach of a restriction against a specific use, e.g. not to use as offices, does not exclude the tenancy from the Act.
- A business use in breach of a restriction against any purposes except a specified purpose, e.g. not to use except as offices, does not exclude the tenancy from the Act.
- A business use in breach of a restriction against a trade, a profession or an employment does take the tenancy outside the Act.
- The business use does not exclude the tenancy from the Act, even though in breach of a prohibition, if the breach has been consented to or acquiesced in.

D'Silva v Lister House Development Ltd (1970)

An unlawful subtenancy was held to be within the protection of the 1954 Act.

There are differences between the meaning of 'consent' and 'acquiescence' in section 24(4) of the 1954 Act.

Bell v Alfred Franks & Barlett Co Ltd (1980)

It was held that in the context of section 23(4) of the 1954 Act, 'acquiescence' meant a passive attitude by a person with knowledge of a breach of a prohibition, 'Consent' involved a positive demonstrative act of an affirmative nature, which could be either in writing, oral or by conduct, but there must be something more than a mere standing by and the absence of objection.

Methodist Secondary Schools Trust Deed Trustees v O'Leary (1993)

A house immediately adjacent to a school was let to the school trustees and occupied by a school caretaker. It was held that the tenancy of the house was not one to which Part II of the 1954 Act applied. The trustees were in breach of the covenant in the lease to use the demised premises for the purpose of a private residence in single occupation only. The landlord neither consented nor acquiesced in the use of the house for such purposes. Knowledge is a prerequisite of acquiescence. The landlord could not be said to have acquiesced in the continuing breach of covenant unless he knew the facts that gave rise to the breach. On the evidence he had not acquiesced in the breach of covenant.

2.8 STATUTORY EXCLUSIONS

Landlord and Tenant Act 1954, section 43

Section 43 contains four exclusions to the general application of the Act to business tenancies:

(1) agricultural holdings and farm business tenancies;
(2) mining leases;
(3) office, appointment or employment; and
(4) term certain of six months.

2.8.1 Agricultural holdings and farm business tenancies

The 1954 Act does not apply to a tenancy of an agricultural holding or a farm business tenancy. An agricultural holding is defined in section 69 of the Act as having the same meaning as in the *Agricultural Holdings Act* 1986.

Gladstone v Bower (1960)

In this case, it was held that the defendant's tenancy for a fixed period of 18 months was an interest greater than a tenancy from year to year within section 2(1) of the *Agricultural Holdings Act* 1948 and was not within the protection of the 1954 Act.

EWP v Moore (1991)

The landlord let a farm of about 120 acres to the tenant for a fixed term of 23 months. The tenant claimed that he was entitled to remain in possession at the end of the term on the ground that the tenancy was a business tenancy within Part II of the 1954 Act and had not been duly terminated. The landlord contended that the tenancy was a tenancy of an agricultural holding within the definition in the *Agricultural Holdings Act* 1986 and was excluded from the protection of the 1954 Act by section 43(1)(a) of the that Act. It was held that the tenancy was not protected under either Act.

2.8.2 Mining leases

The 1954 Act does not apply to a tenancy of a mining lease.

O'Callaghan v Elliott (1965)

It was held that a lease for the working of sand and gravel was outside the 1954 Act.

2.8.3 **Office, appointment or employment**

The 1954 Act does not apply to a tenancy granted because the tenant holds an office, appointment or employment from the landlord which will continue only so long as he remains in that position. If the tenancy was granted after 30 September 1954 (the day before the 1954 Act commenced) there must be a written lease which expresses the purpose of the grant.

2.8.4 **Term certain of six months**

The 1954 Act does not apply to a tenancy for a term certain of six months or less unless there is provision for renewal or extension beyond six months or the tenant has been in occupation for a period which, together with any period of occupation by a predecessor in the business, exceeds 12 months.

Cricket v Shaftesbury plc (1999)

Occupation for two consecutive periods of five months each, together with a further period of occupation as a tenant at will, exceeded 12 months. It did not attract the protection of the Act as a tenancy at will is not a tenancy for the purposes of the Act.

2.8.5 **General points**

Tenancies of on-licensed premises

The *Landlord and Tenant (Licensed Premises) Act* 1990 brought to an end, in phases, the exclusion from protection of tenancies of on-licensed premises. All tenancies of licensed premises entered into after 11 July 1989 enjoy the protection of the 1954 Act. In the case of tenancies granted before 11 July 1989, or granted pursuant to a contract made before that date, the exclusion from protection ceased to have effect on 11 July 1992, if the tenancy was in existence on that date.

The Crown

The 1954 Act binds the Crown subject to certain special statutory provisions.

3
Contracting out

3.1 THE NEW PROCEDURE

Landlord and Tenant Act 1954, section 38(1)

Section 38(1) of the *Landlord and Tenant Act* 1954 ('1954 Act') limits contracting out of Part II of the Act.

The basic principle is that any agreement is void (except as provided by section 38A of the Act) in so far as it purports to preclude an application or request for a new tenancy or provides for the termination or surrender of the tenancy or for any penalty or disability upon such application or request being made.

Landlord and Tenant Act 1954, section 38A

Section 38A(1) relates to agreements between the persons who will be the landlord and the tenant in relation to a tenancy to be granted for a term of years certain which will be a tenancy to which Part II of the Act applies. Such persons may agree that the provisions of sections 24 to 28 of the Act shall be excluded in relation to that tenancy.

The practical effect of section 38A is to remove the requirement that the court should authorise any exclusion by agreement of the provisions of the 1954 Act conferring security of tenure and any agreement to surrender a tenancy subject to the Act. This is subject to procedural requirements.

Landlord and Tenant Act 1954, section 38A(1)

Section 38A(1) provides that an agreement to exclude the provisions of sections 24 to 28 of the Act in relation to the tenancy to be granted for a term of years certain, shall be void unless:

(a) the landlord has served a notice on the tenant in the form, or substantially in the form, set out in Schedule 1 to the *Regulatory Reform (Business Tenancies) (England and Wales) Order* 2003 ('2003 Order'), and

(b) the requirements specified in Schedule 2 of the 2003 Order are met.

Subject to the provisions of paragraph 4 of Schedule 2 of the 2003 Order, the notice referred to in subsection 38A(3)(a) of the 1954 Act must be served not less than 14 days before the tenant enters into the tenancy or becomes contractually bound to do so. The tenant, or a person duly authorised by him, must then, before entering into the tenancy or becoming contractually bound to do so, make a declaration in the form, or substantially in the form, set out in paragraph 7 of Schedule 2 of the 2003 Order.

Paragraph 4 of Schedule 2 covers the position where the 14-day requirement is not met. In such a case, the notice referred to in section 38A(3)(a) of the 1954 Act must be served on the tenant before the tenant enters into the tenancy or becomes contractually bound to do so. Additionally, the tenant must then, also before that time, make a statutory declaration in the form, or substantially in the form, set out in Schedule 2, paragraph 8.

Further requirements include:

■ a reference to the notice referred to in section 38A(3)(a), and to either the tenant's declaration or statutory declaration, must be endorsed on the instrument creating the tenancy (Schedule 2, paragraph 5); and

■ the agreement under section 38A(1), or a reference to that agreement, must also be contained in or endorsed on the instrument creating the tenancy (Schedule 2, paragraph 6).

The procedural requirements of section 38A are complicated and reference should be made to the 2003 Order for the precise procedure to be followed.

Landlord and Tenant Act 1954, section 38A(2)

Section 38A(2) provides that a landlord and tenant in relation to a tenancy and subject to the provisions of the Act may make an agreement to surrender the tenancy. The requirements relating to the making of an effective agreement to surrender are set out in Schedules 3 and 4 to the 2003 Order and are similar to those described above, requiring the service of notice on the tenant and the making of a declaration or statutory declaration by the tenant.

Once again, reference should be made to the 2003 Order for the precise procedure to be followed.

Metropolitan Police District Receiver v Palacegate Properties Ltd (2000)

It was held that a 'term of years' certain includes a tenancy for a term of years which contains a break clause.

Joseph v Joseph (1966)

It was held that an agreement is void by section 38(1) of the 1954 Act if it has the effect of precluding the tenant from exercising his rights under the Act even though it does not expressly provide that such is the purpose.

Allnat London Properties Ltd v Newton (1984)

The tenant covenanted to offer to surrender his tenancy before assigning it. Since the effect of the agreement to surrender in this case would have been to preclude the tenant from applying for a new tenancy under the 1954 Act, the agreement was void and unenforceable. *Joseph v Joseph* (1966), above, was followed.

Tarjomani v Panther Securities Ltd (1983)

An agreement contained in a letter under which the tenant would be released from all outstanding rent and other arrears in consideration of him surrendering his lease was held to be void.

A penalty or disability includes any provision that would have the effect of deterring a tenant from exercising what would otherwise be his rights under Part II of the 1954 Act.

Stevenson and Rush (Holdings) Ltd v Langdon (1978)

In this case, there was a provision in the lease requiring the tenant to pay to the landlord all costs, charges and expenses including legal and surveyor's costs of, and incidental to, the preparation and service of any notice by either party on the other under the 1954 Act and all negotiations subsequent thereto and of all proceedings thereunder and to keep the landlord indemnified against all costs in respect of such notices, negotiations and proceedings. The provision was held to be void since it was the imposition of a penalty on the tenant.

3.2 ASSIGNING A CONTRACTED OUT LEASE

An assignee of a tenancy that is contracted out of the provisions of section 24 to 28 of the 1954 Act, has no greater security of tenure than the original tenant.

Parc Battersea Ltd v Hutchinson PB Ltd (1999)

A lease of premises for a fixed term was excluded from the operation of sections 24 to 28 of the 1954 Act. The tenant sublet part of the premises on a monthly tenancy. It was a term of the subtenancy that it could not be ended until a date later than the date the lease expired. It was held that the subtenancy took effect as an assignment of the remainder of the fixed term of the lease that was excluded from the protection of the 1954 Act. The subtenant had no statutory protection.

3.3 DECIDING WHETHER TO AGREE A CONTRACTED OUT LEASE

Factors to consider when deciding whether or not to agree a contracted out lease include such matters as:

- effect on security of tenure;
- individual business plans and requirements of tenants/ landlords;
- availability of properties in the market/potential tenants;
- effect on terms and rent; and
- compliance with the necessary statutory procedure.

4
Continuation of the tenancy

4.1 NATURE AND PRACTICAL EFFECT OF THE CONTINUATION TENANCY

Landlord and Tenant Act 1954, section 24(1)

Section 24(1) of the *Landlord and Tenant Act* 1954 ('1954 Act') provides that a tenancy to which the 1954 Act applies shall not come to an end unless terminated in accordance with the provisions of Part II of that Act.

General principle

Section 24 contains the fundamental protection that is given to tenants by the 1954 Act. The general principle is that a tenancy that is within the 1954 Act does not come to an end unless it is terminated in accordance with the provisions of Part II of that Act.

At common law, a tenancy may come to an end in a variety of ways. If the contractual term is ended at common law (for example, by a landlord's notice to quit) or by a notice under a break clause in the lease, a tenancy protected by the 1954 Act continues under section 24.

Weinberg's Weatherproof Ltd v Radcliffe Paper Mill Co Ltd (1957)

A lease of rooms contained a break clause on the expiration of the first 7 and 14 years of the term on six months notice to the other side. A break clause notice was served on the tenants. It was held that the notice was effective to cut down the term demised by the lease and the tenants were holding over merely by virtue of the 1954 Act. The landlords could, however, at any time serve a statutory notice under section

25 of the Act, and the tenants could at any time apply for a new tenancy under section 26.

Scholl Manufacturing Co Ltd v Clifton (Slim Line) (1966)

A lease contained a break clause that provided that either party could determine the lease on 25 March 1966 by giving the other six months previous notice in writing. On 11 May 1965, the landlord served upon the tenant a notice under section 25 terminating the tenancy on 25 March 1966. The Court of Appeal held that 'notice to quit' within section 69 of the 1954 Act included a notice pursuant to a break clause. As the date specified in the section 25 notice complied with the terms of the contract and the requirements of the Act, the notice was a good notice effective to bring the contractual term to an end and to terminate the tenancy in accordance with the Act.

A tenancy that continues under section 24 of the 1954 Act is not purely a contractual tenancy, the contractual term having ended. Neither does it have the same legal nature as a Rent Act statutory tenancy.

HL Bolton Engineering Co Ltd v TJ Graham and Sons Ltd (1957)

Lord Justice Denning described the effect of section 24 of the 1954 Act as being to continue the tenant's common law tenancy with a statutory variation as to the mode of determination.

The terms of the contractual tenancy, except those terms concerning termination by the landlord that are inconsistent with the statutory continuation, continue to have effect.

Poster v Slough Estates Ltd (1968)

The tenant is entitled to the same premises as were comprised in the original tenancy during its statutory continuation unless there was a right to remove some part of the premises during the original contractual period.

Whether a guarantee or similar obligation ends on the contractual term date or continues during the statutory continuation under section 24(1) of the 1954 Act.

GMS Syndicate Ltd v Gary Elliot Ltd and others (1981)

A covenant by subtenants to perform the covenants in the sublease 'thenceforth during the residue of the term granted by the sub-lease' meant that the obligation did not expire at the end of their contractual term but continued during the period of statutory continuation under section 24(1) of the 1954 Act.

Junction Estates Ltd v Cope (1974)

A lease for a seven-year term of business premises contained a covenant by the tenant to pay the rent reserved. The defendants joined in the lease as guarantors. The tenant assigned its interest in the lease. The assignee tenant held over on a continuation tenancy under Part II of the 1954 Act. It failed to pay the rent. In an action against the guarantors, it was claimed that they were liable as guarantors for the unpaid rent. It was held that the guarantors' covenant in the lease guaranteed the performance of the obligation to pay the rent reserved by the lease during its term and did not cover any obligation of the tenant to pay rent during any statutory extension of the term.

A Plesser & Co Ltd v Davis (1983)

It was held that the obligation of the guarantor did not extend to the payment of rent for the nine months during which the lease continued under section 24 of the 1954 Act. It was suggested that if it was desired that the guarantor's obligations should extend to the statutory continuation of the tenancy, some such wording as 'or any statutory continuation thereof' should be included in the guarantee covenant.

As a tenancy within the 1954 Act has the potential to continue beyond the contractual term date, a subtenancy created out of it to last beyond that date does not operate as an assignment.

William Skelton & Sons v Harrison and Pinder Ltd (1975)

The underlease of business premises was for a longer term than the head lease but this did not operate as an assignment. This was because the term of the head lease would, by operation of Part II of the 1954 Act, continue indefinitely until terminated by notice in accordance with that Act.

If the original tenant covenanted to pay rent only during the contractual term, and assigned his lease, the landlord cannot recover from him rent payable during the continuation of the tenancy under section 24 of the 1954 Act.

City of London Corporation v Fell (1993)

A lease of business premises was granted for the term of ten years. The defendant tenants, with the landlord's consent, assigned the lease to a company for the remainder of the unexpired term. The term of the lease expired but the assignee company remained in occupation under Part II of the 1954 Act. It surrendered the premises owing a substantial amount of unpaid rent. Proceedings were issued against the defendants, as the original lessees, for the outstanding rent. It was held that the defendants were not contractually bound to pay any rent for the period after expiry of the defendants' ten-year contractual term.

New Zealand Government Property Corporation Ltd v HM & S Ltd (1982)

If a tenancy continues under section 24(1) of the 1954 Act and then the tenancy is surrendered by operation of law when the tenant is granted a new tenancy, the tenant, so long as he remains in possession, does not lose his rights to remove tenant's fixtures added during the old tenancy.

4.2 PRESERVATION OF FORFEITURE AND OTHER COMMON LAW METHODS OF TERMINATION

There are exceptions to the above principle. There are ways in which a tenancy can come to an end apart from the statutory methods of termination. Forfeiture and other common law methods of termination have been preserved.

Landlord and Tenant Act 1954, section 24(2)

Section 24(2) provides that the provisions of section 24(1) shall not prevent the coming to an end of a tenancy by notice to quit given by the tenant, by surrender or forfeiture of a superior tenancy.

It provides that a tenancy may be ended by:

- a notice to quit given by the tenant;
- a surrender; or
- forfeiture, including forfeiture of a superior tenancy,

unless, in the case of a notice to quit, the notice was given before the tenant had been in occupation in right of the tenancy for one month.

4.2.1 Surrender

There must be either a valid express surrender of the lease by deed, or an immediate surrender by operation of law.

Tarjomani v Panther Securities Ltd (1983)

In this case, the landlord and the tenant made an arrangement which was put in the form of a letter from the tenant countersigned by the landlord, which stated that the tenant would be released from all outstanding rent and other arrears 'in consideration of the surrender of the (lease) taking place today ...'. It was held that there was no valid express surrender or surrender by operation of law.

4.2.2 Forfeiture

Meadows v Clerical Medical and General Life Assurance Society (1981)

Where a landlord has taken steps to forfeit a tenancy but an application for relief against forfeiture is expeditiously pursued, the tenancy does not come to an end so as to preclude the tenant from making a valid application to the court for a new tenancy under section 24(1) of the 1954 Act.

Cadogan v Dimovic (1984)

Section 24(2) of the 1954 Act does not prevent an under-lessee, where the underlease is forfeited in consequence of the forfeiture of a superior lease, from applying for relief under section 146(4) of the *Law of Property Act* 1925 by way of the grant of a new lease for the appropriate term.

Hill v Griffin (1987)

The superior tenancy of business premises had been forfeited. The question was whether relief against forfeiture should be granted to the business subtenant. It was held that there was jurisdiction, to grant a monthly tenancy by way of relief to the business subtenant. However, relief from forfeiture was not granted as on the facts the subtenant was not prepared to enter into repairing obligations to the same extent as under the forfeited lease.

4.3 WHAT HAPPENS WHEN BUSINESS USER CEASES

Landlord and Tenant Act 1954, section 24(3)

Section 24(3) provides that:

(a) Where a tenancy to which Part II of the 1954 Act applies ceases to be such a tenancy, it does not end by reason only of the cesser. If it was granted for a term of years certain and has been continued by section 24(1) then (without prejudice to its termination in accordance with the terms of the tenancy) the landlord can terminate it by giving not less than three and not more than six months' notice in writing to the tenant.

(b) Where, at a time when a tenancy is not one to which Part II of the Act applies, the landlord gives notice to quit, the operation of the notice shall not be affected by reason that the tenancy becomes one to which this part of the Act applies after the giving of the notice. Therefore the tenant cannot defeat the landlord's notice to quit by bringing the tenancy within the Act, for example, starting a business use before the tenancy expires.

The landlord in section 24(3)(b) means the immediate landlord. See section 44(2).

Section 24(3)(a) probably only applies when the tenancy ceases to be one to which Part II of the Act applies after the commencement of the statutory continuation under section 24(1) and prior to the application to the court for a new tenancy.

William Skelton & Son Ltd v Harrison & Pinder Ltd (1975)

This case is an example of section 24(3) of the 1954 Act coming into operation on account of the severance of the reversion.

Brown v Jamieson (1959)

It was held that section 24(3)(b) applied to preserve the validity of a notice to quit when the tenancy in question came within the 1954 Act after service of but before expiry of the notice to quit on account of the decontrol of Rent Act protected tenancies by the *Rent Act* 1957.

The tenancy must remain one to which Part II of the 1954 Act applies throughout the period of the proceedings on the application for a new tenancy in order for the tenant to obtain an order for the grant of a new tenancy from the court.

Pulleng v Curran (1980)

In this case, the premises consisted of a grocer's shop and dairyman's shop with a room at the back, a kitchen on the ground floor and residential accommodation above. The landlord served a notice under section 25 of the 1954 Act to terminate the tenancy. The tenant contended that his business use had ceased so that he had become protected by the *Rent Act* 1977. The judge found that the business use had not ceased. A small amount of business use sufficed. The Court of Appeal held that whether business use of the premises had ceased was a question of fact and that the judge had been entitled to reach the conclusion he did.

Morrison Holdings Ltd v Manders Property (Wolverhampton) Ltd (1976)

Leased shop premises were seriously damaged by fire so that the tenants were obliged to vacate them. The landlords operated a break clause in the lease. The tenants applied to the court for a new tenancy. Throughout, they reiterated their intention to return to the premises as soon as they had been rendered fit for occupation. They left certain fixtures and fittings in the premises and retained the keys. The Court of Appeal held that the application for a new tenancy had been validly made. In order to apply for a new tenancy under the 1954 Act, the tenant must show that he is continuing in occupation of the premises for the purpose of a business carried on by him, or, if events over which he has no control have led him to absent himself from the premises, that he continues to exert and claim his rights to occupation. The tenants in this case satisfied the second limb of the test.

Demetriouv v Poolaction Ltd (1991)

This case concerned the continuity of the business tenancy if the tenant vacates because of the need to make repairs that are the landlord's liability.

Flairline Properties Ltd v Hassan (1999)

The tenant of restaurant premises ceased use of one of the restaurant premises following a serious fire. Because of difficulties relating to the obtaining of planning permission, the landlord was unable to reinstate the premises. Meanwhile, the tenant took a lease of other premises nearby and opened a restaurant. When the contractual terms of the original leases expired, the landlord claimed possession on the basis that the tenant was not in occupation for the purposes of section 23 of the 1954 Act. The claim was dismissed. The tenant, having absented himself from the premises since the fire because of events over which he had no control, continued to exert and claim his right of occupancy up to the contractual term date of his leases, and beyond.

4.4 ANCILLARY PROVISIONS

Landlord and Tenant Act 1954, section 27

Section 27 provides two methods by which a tenant for a fixed term may terminate his tenancy. This will be appropriate where the tenant does not want his tenancy to continue under the Act and does not want to apply for a new tenancy.

The statutory notices under this section can only be served when the tenancy is for a term certain. A tenant under a periodic tenancy, whether contractual or continued under section 24, may bring his tenancy to an end by means of a notice to quit.

FIRST METHOD

The first method applies where a tenancy for a term certain has not reached its contractual expiry date.

Section 27(1)

Under section 27(1), where the tenant under a tenancy to which Part II of the 1954 Act applies, being a tenancy for a term certain gives to his immediate landlord, not later than three months before the contractual expiry date, a notice in writing that he does not desire his tenancy to be continued under the Act, then the tenancy will not be continued under the Act and will end by effluxion of time on the contractual expiry date.

Section 27(1A)

Section 27(1A) provides that a tenant vacating the property by the expiry of the contractual term of the tenancy brings the tenancy to an end without the need for the service of a section 27(1) notice.

Section 27(1A) is statutory confirmation of the decision of the Court of Appeal in *Esselte AB v Pearl Assurance plc* (1997) and *Single Horse Properties Ltd v Surrey County Council* (2002).

The effect of *Esselte v Pearl Assurance plc* was that, provided the tenant was not in occupation beyond the expiry of the tenancy, the tenancy could not continue under section 24 of the 1954 Act, occupation being an essential ingredient of the protection of the Act.

In *Surrey County Council v Single Horse Properties Ltd,* it was held that if a tenant ceases to occupy the premises before the contractual term date, the fixed-term tenancy will come to an end upon the expiry of the term and section 24(1) will not apply.

SECOND METHOD

The second method applies when the contractual expiry date has passed and the tenancy is continuing under section 24 of the Act.

Section 27(2)

Under section 27(2), the tenancy does not come to an end by reason only of the tenant ceasing to occupy the property comprised in the tenancy. The tenant may end the tenancy by a notice in writing to his immediate landlord, which must have a minimum period between service and expiry of three months.

Neither of the notices under section 27(1) and (2) mentioned above is valid if given before the tenant has been in occupation of the premises in right of the tenancy for at least a month.

Landlord and Tenant Act 1954, section 24(2A) and section 24(2B)

Section 24(2A) provides that neither the tenant nor the landlord may make an application under section 24(1) if the other has made such an application and the application has been served.

Section 24(2B) provides that neither the tenant nor the landlord may make an application under section 24(1) if the landlord has made an application under section 29(2) and the application has been served.

5
First steps: notices and requests

5.1 SECTION 25 NOTICES

The landlord may terminate a tenancy to which Part II of the *Landlord and Tenant Act* 1954 ('1954 Act') applies by a notice under section 25 given to the tenant in the prescribed form specifying the date at which the tenancy is to come to an end ('the date of termination').

5.1.1 Requirements of a section 25 notice

A section 25 notice must:

(a) be given by a competent landlord;
(b) be given to the tenant;
(c) relate to the whole of the property comprised in the tenancy;
(d) specify a date for termination of the tenancy which complies with the requirements of the 1954 Act and of the tenancy;
(e) be in the prescribed form;
(f) state whether the landlord would oppose an application to the court for the grant of a new tenancy, and if so, on which of the statutory grounds he would do so; and
(g) in a case where the landlord does not oppose the grant of a new tenancy, set out the landlord's proposals as to the property to be comprised in the tenancy, the rent payable under the new tenancy and the other terms of the new tenancy.

5.1.2 Content of the notice

Tegerdine v Brooks (1977)

A fish and chip shop was let on a weekly tenancy. The landlord gave notice to the tenant terminating his tenancy, stating that he would not oppose an application for a new tenancy. The notice was in the prescribed form except that some of the notes were omitted. It was held that that the departure from the prescribed form was immaterial to the whole on the facts of the case.

5.1.3 Statement of opposition to a new tenancy

Landlord and Tenant Act 1954, section 25(6)

Section 25(6) provides that a notice under section 25 shall not have effect unless it states whether the landlord is opposed to the grant of a new tenancy to the tenant.

Barclays Bank v Ascott (1961)

The landlords of business premises served a section 25 notice in the prescribed form. The notice stated that the landlords would not oppose an application for a new tenancy provided that the tenant's brother, or some other person approved by the landlords, was a guarantor for payment of the rent and performance and observance of the covenants in the new tenancy. It was held that the notice was invalid. The notice meant the landlords would oppose an application to the court for new tenancy if no suitable guarantor was found. The notice did not specify any ground under section 30(1) of the 1954 Act nor give the tenant sufficient information to enable her to deal, in a proper way, with the situation arising from the notice.

Lewis v MTC (Cars) Ltd (1974)

The landlord set out in the section 25 notice, the grounds for opposing an application as required by section 25(6), but accidentally failed to strike out the first sentence of paragraph 3 of the prescribed form. The result was that the notice as served contained statements that the landlord would not oppose an application and that she would oppose an application. It was held that the notice was valid. By setting forth the landlord's reasons for opposing an application to the court, the notice clearly showed the landlord's intention to oppose an application and was therefore to be construed as stating that the landlord would do so.

5.1.4 Statement of grounds of opposition to a new tenancy

Landlord and Tenant Act 1954, section 25(7)

Section 25(7) provides that a notice under section 25 which states that the landlord is opposed to the grant of a new tenancy shall not have effect unless it also specifies one or more of the grounds specified in section 30(1) of the 1954 Act as the ground or grounds for his opposition.

The landlord is confined by virtue of section 30(1) of the Act to the grounds of opposition specified in his notice when he comes to oppose an application to the court for a new tenancy.

It is enough if the appropriate paragraph in section 30(1) is clearly indicated.

Bolton's (House Furnishers) v Oppenheim (1959)

In this case, a landlord served on his tenants a notice in the prescribed form to terminate a business tenancy under section 25 of the 1954 Act. The landlord's notice did not contain the final words of the in the ground of opposition in section 30(1)(f). However, the notice referred to the back of the form where the grounds of opposition were set out, including the whole of section 30(1)(f). It was held that the notice sufficiently stated the ground of opposition.

The principle is that the landlord's notice must give the tenant clear warning of what the landlord relies on.

Biles v Caesar (1957)

In this case, a notice served under section 25 set out the grounds on which the landlords objected to the granting of a new tenancy under section 30(1)(f) of the 1954 Act. The notice stated that the landlords intended to demolish the whole of the premises. That was incorrect as they intended to demolish a substantial part only. It was held that section 30(1) required the landlords to state on which paragraph of the subsection they relied but not to state on which part of such paragraph they relied.

Marks v British Waterways Board (1963)

The tenant requested a new tenancy under section 26 of the 1954 Act. The landlords said in their counter-notice that it was their intention to demolish the premises in question. In fact, they never did have the intention of demolishing the premises themselves, but their successor in title did have such an intention. The tenant knew what the true situation was and was not deceived. It was held that the counter-notice would not be invalidated by a slip unless it was of such a nature as to make the notice deceptive or misleading or amounted to a material misrepresentation.

Housleys Ltd v Bloomer-Holt Ltd (1966)

It was held that the section 25 notice, although it did not follow precisely the wording of section 30(1)(f) of the 1954 Act, sufficiently revealed on which of the grounds set out in section 30(1) the landlords were relying.

Sevenarts v Busvine (1969)

The landlord did not own the beneficial interest in the head lease of the property. The head lease had been assigned to her because the freeholder was unwilling to permit an assignment to a company of which she was the managing director and major shareholder. A section 25 notice on subtenants stated that the landlord would oppose the grant of a new tenancy under section 30(1)(g) of the 1954 Act (own occupation). This was incorrect. The landlord, although she was the managing director, was not carrying on the business. It was intended that the company, which was already carrying on the business under her management, should carry on business in the whole of the property including the part included in the underlease. The Court of Appeal held that the notice was not a bad notice. No one was misled. The tenants knew what the true situation was. The counter-notice was a good indication that section 30(1)(g) was going to be relied upon. It contained no material misrepresentation.

5.1.5 Requirement to set out proposals

Landlord and Tenant Act 1954, section 25(8)

A notice under section 25 that states that the landlord is not opposed to the grant of a new tenancy to the tenant shall not have effect unless it sets out the landlord's proposals as to:

(a) the property to be comprised in the new tenancy (being either the whole or part of the property comprised in the current tenancy);
(b) the rent to be payable under the new tenancy; and
(c) the other terms of the new tenancy.

The requirement to set out proposals may be interpreted as a requirement to set out genuine and realistic proposals.

It is implicit in the statutory machinery that once a landlord has served a notice he cannot unilaterally withdraw it or amend it or serve a further notice to replace it.

Nursey v P Currie (Dartford) Ltd (1959)

The landlords carried on a garage business in a yard. They granted a tenancy of some of the buildings in the yard. The landlords served a section 25 notice relying on the ground in section 30(1)(g) of the 1954 Act (own occupation) only. The tenants applied for a new tenancy. The landlords were then granted planning permission to develop their premises as a petrol filling station with car park behind it. This involved demolition of the tenant's buildings. It was held that the landlords had not established their opposition under section 30(1)(g) because at the date of the hearing the landlord did not intend to occupy the buildings that were to be demolished. There was no power to amend the section 25 notice to rely on section 25(1)(f) (demolition and reconstruction).

Polyviou v Seeley (1979)

A tenant's request for a tenancy under section 26 cannot be unilaterally withdrawn.

Hutchinson v Lamberth (1984)

A County Court judge, on an application for a new tenancy resisted by the landlord on grounds (a) and (b) of section 30(1) of the 1954 Act, permitted the landlord to amend his answer so as to incorporate ground (c) (allegations of nuisance) even though these grounds had not been specified in the section 25 notice. The Court of Appeal held that the judge had no jurisdiction to permit the amendment, but the amendment, though irregular, was not sufficient to justify a retrial, as the evidence of nuisance was relevant to the exercise of the judge's discretion under grounds (a) and (b) of section 30(1), those grounds being discretionary.

5.1.6 Conflicting notices

Barclays Bank plc v Bee (2001)

The landlord's solicitors served two conflicting notices purportedly under section 25 of the 1954 Act. One notice stated that any application for a new tenancy would be opposed on 'the grounds mentioned in paragraph(s) … of section 30(1)' but did not state the ground or grounds (notice A). The second notice stated that any application for a new tenancy would not be opposed (notice B). The tenant's solicitors sought confirmation that an application for a new tenancy would not be opposed. The landlord's solicitors then served a third notice stating that any application would be opposed on grounds (f) and (g) of section 30(1) (notice C).

It was held that a reasonable recipient of the letter containing the two notices (A and B) would not ignore what was stated in notice A. The notices did not unambiguously inform the recipient of the landlord's intention. Having regard to their inconsistency, neither notice A or B were valid. Notice C was the only valid notice.

5.1.7 **Time for service**

There is a time limit, applicable to all notices that the notice must be given not more than twelve months and not less than six months before the date for the termination of the tenancy that it specifies. There is a second time limit that differs according to whether the tenancy is for a term certain or is a period tenancy. The principle is that a tenancy cannot be ended by notice before it would have been ended at common law. Therefore, in the case of a term certain, the notice must not specify a date of termination that is earlier than the date on which the tenancy would have come to an end by effluxion of time (i.e. the contractual term date). In the case of a periodic tenancy, the date specified for termination must not be earlier than the date on which the tenancy would have been brought to an end by a notice to quit served at the same date as the statutory notice.

Landlord and Tenant Act 1954, section 25(1)

Section 25(1) provides that the landlord may terminate a tenancy to which the Act applies by a notice given to the tenant in the prescribed form specifying the date at which the tenancy is to come to an end (the 'date of termination').

Landlord and Tenant Act 1954, section 25(2)

Section 25(2) provides that subject to the provisions of section 25(3), a notice under section 25 shall not have effect unless it is given not more than twelve months and not less than six months before the date of termination specified in the notice.

Landlord and Tenant Act 1954, section 25(3)

Section 25(3) provides that in the case of a tenancy which, apart from the provisions of the Act, could have been brought to an end by a notice to quit given by the landlord:

(a) the date of termination specified in a notice under this section shall not be earlier than the earliest date on which, apart from Part II of the Act, the tenancy could have been brought to an end by notice to quit by the landlord on the date of the giving of the notice under this section; and

(b) where, apart from Part II of the Act, more than six months' notice to quit would have been required to bring the tenancy to an end, section 25(2) shall have effect with the substitution for twelve months of a period of six months longer than the length of the notice to quit which would have been required.

Landlord and Tenant Act 1954, section 25(4)

Section 25(4) provides that in the case of any other tenancy, a notice under section 25 shall not specify a date of termination earlier than the date on which, apart from Part II of the Act, the tenancy would have come to an end by effluxion of time.

When a tenancy runs from a certain day it ends at midnight of the appropriate anniversary of that day. A notice that specifies that anniversary as the date of termination is accordingly valid under section 25(4).

Re Crowhurst Park, Sims-Hilditch v Simmons (1974)

In this case, the tenancy came 'to an end by effluxion of time', within section 25(4), on 25 December 1972. Accordingly, when the defendant gave notice to the plaintiff terminating the tenancy on 25 December 1972 he was referring to a date on which, apart from the 1954 Act, the tenancy would have come to an end by effluxion of time. The notice was therefore not invalid under section 25(4).

Bowes-Lyon v Green (1963)

The tenancy may be one to which Part II of the 1954 Act applies (e.g. because the tenant occupies part of the demised premises with only a part sublet). Even if its term is less than 14 months off it will not end by effluxion of time within that period since it will be continued by section 24 of the Act.

Timing is important where there is a tenant and a subtenant protected by the 1954 Act. The circumstances may be such that the superior landlord will only become the competent landlord in relation to the subtenant by serving notice on the head tenant.

If the landlord posts off both section 25 notices on the same day, the resulting position is not free from argument.

Keith Bayley Rogers & Co v Cubes Ltd (1975)

Templeman J said that it was to be assumed that the notices were delivered in the correct sequence, i.e. on the intermediate tenant first and then on the subtenant.

5.2 WHO TO SERVE

5.2.1 Meaning of 'the landlord'

'The landlord' is not necessarily the tenant's immediate landlord but is the person who, at the time the matter is being considered, fulfils the conditions set out in section 44 of the 1954 Act.

Landlord and Tenant Act 1954, section 44(1)

Section 44 deals with the situation where there are a number of tenancies and subtenancies carved out of the freehold. There are a number of provisions in the Act concerning acts taken by or in relation to a landlord (e.g. a landlord's notice under section 25 and tenant's request under section 26). Where there is only a freeholder and a tenant of the premises, then the landlord is the freeholder. Where there is a chain of tenancies, it is necessary to ascertain which of the persons with an interest superior to the tenancy in question is the landlord for the purposes of the statutory provisions. By subsection (1) the answer is to enquire into which of the interests superior to the tenancy in question is the lowest in the chain of interests yet fulfils the following conditions:

(a) it will not come to an end within 14 months by effluxion of time, and

(b) no notice has been sent to bring it to an end within 14 months or within any further period of interim continuation under the Act.

For this purpose, the owner of the interest that satisfies the conditions is the landlord. The person who is the landlord at any time is usually called 'the competent landlord'.

Landlord and Tenant Act 1954, section 44(1A)

Section 44(1A) deals with the position where the reversion to a tenancy protected by the Act is owned by different persons. The landlords of parts of premises let together on a tenancy protected by the 1954 Act may come together for the purposes of that Act (e.g. by jointly serving a section 25 notice).

Landlord and Tenant Act 1954, section 44(2)

The definition of the landlord in section 44(1) applies generally to the use of the term 'the landlord' in Part II of the Act, except that a reference to a notice to quit given by the landlord is always a reference to a notice given by the immediate landlord (section 44(2)).

5.2.2 Change of landlord

There can only be one person who is the landlord at any one time in relation to a tenancy. However, the nature of the definition is such that events can occur at any time to change the person who is the landlord.

AD Wimbush & Son Ltd v Franmills Properties Ltd and others (1961)

The landlord of business premises served a notice under section 25 of the 1954 Act terminating a business tenancy. The notice was in the prescribed form and stated that the landlords would oppose an application for a new tenancy, the ground of opposition being that provided in section 30(1)(g) (own occupation). The tenants notified the landlord that they were not willing to give up possession and applied to the court for a new tenancy. The application having not yet been determined, there was a change of landlord. It was not in dispute that the new landlord had the intention required by section 30(1)(g), but the question arose as to whether the new landlord was entitled to rely on the notice and on the ground of opposition since, although it was landlord at the date of the hearing, it was not the landlord at the date the notice was given. It was held that the new landlord was entitled to rely on the notice:

- the reference to the landlord in the statement of the ground of opposition referred to whomsoever was the opposing landlord at the hearing of the application for a new tenancy, and
- section 30(1)(g) required the person who at the date of the hearing was the landlord to have the intent specified in paragraph (g).

5.2.3 Change of landlord during court proceedings

If the identity of the competent landlord changes during the course of the court proceedings, the new landlord should be made a party to the proceedings.

Parsons and another v George and another (2004)

The executors of the original landlord served a section 25 notice on the tenants. Shortly afterwards the freehold of the premises was transferred to P. The tenants were informed of this. They applied for a new tenancy. The executors were named as the respondent. The executors acknowledged service and stated that they would object to the grant of a new tenancy because they were not the competent landlord under the 1954 Act. It was held that it is possible to interpret rule 19.5(1)(c) of the *Civil Procedure Rules* 1998 ('CPR') as referring to any enactment that allows, or does not prohibit, a change of parties following the relevant limitation period. Section 29(3) of the 1954 Act does not prohibit changes of party after the expiry of the time limit. CPR 19.5(3)(b) was satisfied in this case because the tenants had always intended to claim a new tenancy from the competent landlord. Their mistake had been one that fell within this paragraph. The court exercised its discretion to allow the substitution. The error was obvious and the amendment would not cause the true competent landlord any prejudice.

Piper v Muggleton (1956)

A was the landlord for the purposes of Part II of the 1954 Act when the tenant, B, made an application for a new tenancy. A ceased to be a landlord within section 44 when he became a statutory tenant under the *Rent Act* 1977, as he did not then own an interest in the premises. Thereafter, the proceedings for a new tenancy were not properly constituted. The proceedings were remitted to the County Court for a re-hearing after B had joined the superior landlord as respondent to the application for a new tenancy.

Where the reversionary interest is held by joint tenants in law they must both be named in the section 25 notice.

Pearson v Alyo (1990)

In this case, a notice purporting to be given under section 25 stated the name of a husband only although he and his wife were registered at the Land Registry as joint freehold owners. The property was a hotel and had been purchased by the husband with his own money but he had had the name of his wife added on his solicitor's advice because of advantages to his wife if he predeceased her.

It was held that the notice was invalid. A notice under section 25 must give a tenant the information necessary to enable him to avail himself of his statutory rights. The necessary information included the identity of his landlord. The expression 'the landlord' in this case meant the husband and the wife together.

5.2.4 **Receivers and managers**

Landlord and Tenant Act 1954, section 67

Section 67 provides for the case where the interest of the landlord is subject to a mortgage and the mortgagee is in possession, or a receiver has been appointed.

Meah v Mouskos (1964)

In such circumstances, it is the mortgagee or receiver who is 'the landlord' for the purposes of the 1954 Act.

5.2.5 **Trustees**

Where the legal estate is held on trust, the trustees are the landlord and not the beneficiaries under the trust: *Dun & Bradstreet (Software Services England) Ltd v Provident Mutual Life Assurance Association* (1998).

Outside the special provisions of section 41A of the 1954 Act, all joint tenants should join together in the giving of notices: *Harris v Black* (1983).

Booth v Reynolds (1974)

A husband and wife were joint tenants of business premises. The husband carried on business alone as he and his wife had separated. The landlord's section 25 notice was addressed to and served on the husband only. It was held that the section 25 notice was invalid as it had to be addressed to all persons who constituted the tenant. Section 25 notice could not be validated by section 41A of the 1954 Act as the husband and wife had never carried on business in partnership.

Where there are chains of tenancies, this may create complications affecting the machinery of the 1954 Act.

Section 65 of the Act contains provisions as to reversions and Schedule 6 contains provisions for the purposes of Part II where the immediate landlord is not the freeholder.

5.3 HOW TO SERVE

Landlord and Tenant Act 1954, section 66(4)

Section 66(4) provides that section 23 of the *Landlord and Tenant Act* 1927 ('1927 Act') shall apply for the purposes of the 1954 Act.

Landlord and Tenant Act 1927, section 23

Section 23 of the 1927 Act provides that:

> 'Any notice ... under this Act shall be in writing and may be served on the person on whom it is to be served either personally, or by leaving it for him at his last known place of abode in England and Wales, or by sending it through the post in a registered letter addressed to him there ...'.

As a result of the *Recorded Delivery Service Act* 1962, the same effect as was given by that section to a registered letter now falls to be given to a letter dispatched by the recorded delivery service.

Service will be good if the notice is left at the 'last known place of abode' of the tenant, which can include a business address, and service in accordance with section 23 of the 1927 Act will be good even if the notice is never received.

Italica Holdings SA Bayadea (1985)

The landlords sent a section 25 notice to the tenant by recorded delivery post. The tenant claimed that no notice was given to him. The court rejected this contention. A notice in the proper form was addressed to the tenant at the hotel that was the subject of the action. Although not received by the tenant, it had been left at his 'last known place of abode' within the meaning of section 23 of the 1927 Act, which was applied to notices under the 1954 Act. 'Place of abode' could include a business address. Secondly, there was evidence which justified the inference that the section 25 notice had in fact reached the tenant's authorised agent at the hotel and had been transmitted to the tenants then solicitors.

Blunden v Frogmore Investments Ltd (2003)

Bomb damage rendered business premises unfit for occupation. The landlord served a break notice and also a section 25 notice. The notices were sent by recorded delivery to the last known residential address of the tenant. The notices were also affixed to the door of the demised premises, which were inaccessible due to bomb damage. The tenant did not receive the notices. There was a clause in the lease providing that notice was validly served if sent to the tenant by post at the tenant's last known address in Great Britain, or if served under section 196(1) of the *Law of Property Act* 1925. It was held that the section 25 notice operated as an effective break clause notice and was validly served. It was validly served under the terms of the lease. It was also validly served under section 23(1) of the 1927 Act.

Notices served by recorded delivery are deemed to be served when posted.

Beanby Estates Ltd v Egg Stores (Stamford Hill) Ltd (2003)

The landlord sent a section 25 notice by recorded delivery post to the tenant. The tenant served a counter-notice and applied for a new tenancy. Under section 29(2) of the 1954 Act, that application had to be made within four months of the service of the section 25 notice. The tenant said the application for the new tenancy had been made in time because the section 25 notice was served when it was received. The landlord said it was out of time because a notice served by recorded delivery was deemed received on the date of posting. It was held that service is deemed made on the date upon which the notice had been put in the post for recorded delivery and not the date of actual receipt.

CA Webber (Transport) Ltd v Railtrack plc (2003)

The claimant tenant held two business tenancies from the defendant landlord. The landlord sent to the tenant, notices under section 25 of the 1954 Act, by recorded delivery. The notices were sent on a Friday. Because the tenant had an arrangement with the Post Office not to have mail delivered on a Saturday, it received the documents on the following Monday or Tuesday. The tenant contended that the notices were invalid because they were served less than six months before the termination date specified in the notices. The Court of Appeal held that where a notice is served by a primary method authorised by section 23 of the 1927 Act, for example by recorded delivery, it is immaterial whether the notice is received. The date of service is the date upon which the server puts the notice in the post. The expression 'sending through the post' in section 23 of the 1927 Act cannot be construed as requiring an attempt to deliver or actual delivery. The construction of section 23 that was adopted by the court did not infringe section 3 of the *Human Rights Act* 1998.

Chiswell v Griffon Land and Estates Ltd (1975)

The landlord's solicitors served on the tenant a notice under section 25 of the 1954 Act terminating his tenancy of certain business premises. Within two months of the date of the service of the section 25 notice, the tenant's solicitors wrote to the landlord's solicitors notifying them of the tenant's unwillingness to give up possession. The letter was sent by ordinary post, but was never received by the landlord's solicitors. The Court of Appeal held that the words 'duly notified' in section 29(2) of the Act referred back to the requirements contained in section 25(5). They required the tenant to notify the landlord in writing whether or not he was willing to give up possession of the property comprised in the tenancy within the two-month period. As the tenant had not complied with that requirement, the court had no power under section 29(2) to entertain his application for a new tenancy.

The notice was neither sent by registered post nor recorded delivery service. Accordingly section 23 of the 1927 Act did not apply.

5.4 SECTION 26 REQUEST BY THE TENANT

Landlord and Tenant Act 1954, section 26(1)

Section 26(1) provides that a tenant's request for a new tenancy may be made where the current tenancy is a tenancy granted for a term of years certain exceeding one year, whether or not continued by section 24 of the 1954 Act, or granted for a term of years certain and thereafter from year to year.

Polyviou v Seeley (1979)

The Court of Appeal held that once a tenant had made a valid request for a new tenancy specifying the commencement date of the new tenancy, he could not withdraw it and serve a fresh request at a later date. This was because once a valid request had been served, section 26(5) of the 1954 Act operated to determine the current tenancy immediately before the date specified for commencement of the new tenancy, unless the tenant, within the time prescribed by section 29(3) of that Act, applied to the court for a new tenancy. Since the tenant in this case had failed to apply to the court within the prescribed time, he had lost the right to apply to the court for a new tenancy and could not withdraw the first request and make a second request in order to apply to the court within the time which would be the prescribed time were the second request valid.

Sun Life Assurance plc v Thales Tracs Ltd (2001)

The Court of Appeal held that a tenant of business premises was not required to have a genuine intention to take up a new tenancy when making a request for such a tenancy under section 26 of the 1954 Act. Such a conclusion gave effect to the ordinary meaning of the words 'request' and 'proposals' in section 26. A request was an act of asking for something and a proposal was something that had been put forward for consideration. The meaning of request or proposal had to be judged objectively, and the state of mind of the person making them was irrelevant to their meaning. The evidence of the tenant's state of mind when he served a request was inadmissible.

5.4.1 **Content of the request**

The tenant's request for a new tenancy must:

(a) be in the prescribed form; and
(b) set out the tenant's proposals as to the property, rent and other terms of the new tenancy requested.

Landlord and Tenant Act 1954, section 26(3)

Section 26(3) provides that a tenant's request for a new tenancy shall not have effect unless it is made by notice in the prescribed form given to the landlord and sets out the tenant's proposals as to the property to be comprised in the new tenancy (being either the whole or part of the property comprised in the current tenancy), as to the rent to be payable under the new tenancy and as to the other terms of the new tenancy.

The duration of the new tenancy proposed is one of the other terms.

Sidney Bolsom Investment Trust Ltd v Karmios (1956)

A lease of business premises was for the term of seven years. The tenants serviced a section 26 notice requesting a new tenancy stating:

> '… our proposals as to the rent to be payable under the new tenancy and as to the other terms of the new tenancy are an annual rent of £200 per annum upon the terms of the current tenancy as set out in the lease …'.

It was held that the request was valid. Although section 26(3) required that a request under section 26(1) should specify the duration of the new tenancy, this request did comply with that requirement as the words therein 'upon the terms of the current tenancy' imported the duration of the former tenancy (i.e. seven years).

5.4.2 **Time for making the request**

Landlord and Tenant Act 1954, section 26(2)

Section 26(2) provides that the tenant's request for a new tenancy shall be for a tenancy beginning with a date not more than twelve or less than six months after the making of the request. The date specified must not be earlier than the date on which, apart from the 1954 Act, the current tenancy would come to an end by effluxion of time or could be brought to an end by notice to quit given by the tenant.

The tenant's request for a new tenancy must comply with the time limits set out in section 26. A failure to comply with the time limits in section 26(2) means that the tenant's request for a new tenancy will be invalid.

Nevertheless, the time limit provisions are procedural in nature and non-compliance is capable of being waived by the landlord.

Bristol Cars Ltd v RKH Hotels Ltd (1979)

A request for a new tenancy was invalid for failure to comply with the time limit provisions. An application to the court for a new tenancy was made in May 1976. The landlords did not take the point that the request was invalid until April 1977. It was held that by that date their conduct, including negotiations on the terms of a new tenancy and in particular an application made by them to the court to fix an interim rent under section 24A of the 1954 Act, amounted to waiver of the defects in the request. Alternatively, the landlords were estopped from relying upon the defects.

Garston v Scottish Windows Fund (1998)

It was held that section 26 did not empower the tenant to request a new tenancy at the same time as exercising his power under a break clause to bring the old tenancy to an end. Accordingly, the purported request for a new tenancy under section 26 was invalid because the date specified in it for the commencement of the new tenancy was earlier than the date on which the existing tenancy would come to an end by effluxion of time.

5.4.3 **How and to whom a request should be made**

Landlord and Tenant Act 1954, section 26(4)

If the tenant has made a request for a new tenancy under section 26, the landlord cannot thereafter give a notice under section 25 nor can the tenant give a notice under section 27 nor a notice to quit. If the landlord has given notice under section 25, or the tenant has given a notice under section 27, or a notice to quit, then the tenant cannot thereafter make a request under section 26. The object is to ensure that once the landlord or the tenant has taken the appropriate step to end the current tenancy no other step for the same purpose can be taken.

Landlord and Tenant Act 1954, section 26(6)

Within two months of a tenant's request for a new tenancy, the landlord can give a counter-notice that he will oppose the grant of a new tenancy and the grounds of opposition. The landlord will only be able to oppose an application for a new tenancy if he has given a counter-notice and will be confined by section 30(1) to the grounds of opposition in the counter-notice.

XL Fisheries Ltd v Leeds Corp (1955)

A person who acquires the landlord's interest before the two-month period has expired may serve a counter-notice.

Such a person will probably be bound by the terms of any counter-notice served by his predecessor in title.

Stylo Shoes Ltd v Prices Tailors Ltd (1959)

The tenant's request is made and the two-month period begins to run when the request is received by the landlord.

Landlord and Tenant Act 1954, section 26(5)

Section 26(5) provides that where the tenant makes a request for a new tenancy, the current tenancy shall, subject to some other the provisions of the 1954 Act, terminate immediately before the date specified in the request for the beginning of the new tenancy.

5.4.4 Investigations and tactics

Landlord and Tenant Act 1954, section 40

Section 40 of the 1954 Act provides for duties of tenants and landlords of business premises to give information to each other.

Section 40(1) and (3) imposes duties to provide specified information in writing.

Section 40(5) provides that a duty imposed is:

- a duty to give the information concerned within the period of one month beginning with the date of service of the notice;
- if within the period of six months beginning with the date of the service of the notice, that person becomes aware that any information which has been given in pursuance of the notice is not, or is no longer correct, to give the appropriate person correct information within the period of one month beginning with the date on which he becomes aware.

Landlord and Tenant Act 1954, section 40A

Section 40A provides for duties in transfer cases – where a person who has served a notice or on whom a notice has been served has transferred his interest in the premises or any part of it to some other person.

Landlord and Tenant Act 1954, section 40B

Section 40B makes provision for proceedings for breach of duties to give information.

The service of a section 40 notice is an indication that the landlord or tenant has it in mind subsequently to serve a section 25 notice or make a section 26 request based on the information provided. This warning may remind the recipient of the notice of his own rights under the Act and enable him to get in first with his own notice or request. On the other hand, the advantages to be obtained from the service of a formal section 40 notice are considerable and there may be no other practical way of obtaining the information. The effect of the service of the notice may be to force the landlord or the tenant to make admissions about their positions by which they will be bound.

6
Making an application to court

6.1 APPLICATION FOR A NEW TENANCY

A tenant of business premises has a right to seek and obtain the grant of a new tenancy to follow the determination of the current tenancy. The tenant obtains his new tenancy by either applying to the court for it himself or by the landlord applying for it. They can only make an application if either the landlord has terminated the current tenancy by a notice served under section 25 of the *Landlord and Tenant Act* 1954 ('1954 Act') or the tenant has terminated the current tenancy by a request for a new tenancy under section 26 of that Act.

■ The tenant can apply for a new tenancy, under section 29(1), provided that either he has been served with a notice pursuant to section 25 or he has served a request pursuant to section 26.

■ The landlord may commence proceedings for:

– an order for a new tenancy, under section 24(1), if he does not oppose its grant (and provided that either he has served a section 25 notice or has been served with a section 26 request); or

– an order to terminate the continuation tenancy without the grant of a new tenancy, under section 29(2), if he has given a 'hostile' section 25 notice, by which he opposes the grant of a new tenancy or if the tenant has served a section 26 request and the landlord has given a hostile counter-notice under section 26(6), again indicating that he opposes a new tenancy.

■ There is no provision for successive applications. Neither landlord nor tenant may make an application to the court for a new tenancy if the other party has already done so and has served that application.

■ The landlord may not withdraw an application unless the tenant consents to its withdrawal.

- There is no restriction on the tenant's right to withdraw its application. The court will dismiss an application by the landlord under section 25(1) if the tenant informs the court that it does not want a new tenancy.

6.2 JURISDICTION

The application must be issued in the County Court save in exceptional circumstances (complex disputes of fact or points of law of general importance).

6.3 TIME LIMITS

The applications are governed by strict time limits, which the parties and their advisers should be astute to comply with. Section 29A(2) of the 1954 Act provides that the court 'shall not entertain' an application for a new tenancy after the end of the 'statutory period'. This is the period ending either on the date specified in the landlord's section 25 notice or immediately before the date specified in the tenant's section 26 request.

However, section 29B of the Act allows parties to agree to extend time limits for an application to the court if:

- the parties can make an initial agreement before the end of the 'statutory period'; and
- the parties can make one or more further agreements before the previous agreement expires.

There is no time limit set in the 1954 Act in relation to how long or short the extension agreed upon may be nor in relation to the number of extensions which may be agreed. However, extensions must be in writing (section 69(2)) and it is probably the case that general extensions of time may not be agreed.

EJ Riley Investments Ltd v Eurostile Holdings Ltd (1985)

Application made exactly two months after the giving of the section 25 notice was valid.

Kammins Ballrooms v Zenith Investments (1971)

Time requirements of section 29(3) of the 1954 Act for making the application were only procedural and failure to observe a time limit is an irregularity which is capable of being waived by the landlord.

An application made prematurely (or late) 'shall not be entertained by the Court'.

Aly v Aly (1983)

An application is 'made' when the applicant has done everything required of him and when it is received by the court office, not when the application is subsequently issued by the court.

Hodgson v Armstrong (1967)

An application, posted a few days before the expiry of the four-month period to a County Court which was closed for Easter, was 'made' when the post office received the application because the County Court, by instructing the post office to hold over mail during the period of closure, had designated the post office as its agent to keep the mail on its behalf.

Harris v Black (1983)

The court has discretion to make an order at the suit of a trustee to compel his co-trustee to join him in making an application to the court for a new tenancy. On the facts, the order was not granted: the defendant had a larger beneficial interest in the premises than the claimant and was unwilling to incur the financial and other commitments which would be involved in a new lease – there were no special circumstances to justify the making of the order.

Meadows v Clerical Medical and General Life Assurance Society (1981)

Application made before current tenancy was forfeited, will be adjourned (rather than struck out) pending the outcome of any application for relief from forfeiture, because until then the tenancy cannot be said to be dead beyond hope of resurrection.

6.4 SAVING APPLICATIONS

Provided the application has been validly brought, errors can be amended.

Gregson v Channel 4 Television Corporation (2000)

Amendment allowed where the defendant to the proceedings was wrongly named as 'Channel 4 Television Company Limited'. The court found that the mistake was a genuine one and not one which would cause reasonable doubt as to the identity of the party in question.

De Costa v Chartered Society of Queen Square (1961)

Amendment allowed to alter the particulars of the nature of the tenant's business and the description of the parts of the premises occupied by him.

Bar v Pathwood (1987)

Amendment allowed to clarify the original description of what the 'holding' comprised.

Meah v Mouskos (1964)

If the proceedings are improperly constituted, the court has no jurisdiction to grant a new tenancy. Care should be taken to name the correct parties to the application.

Where, after the proceedings are issued, a person other than the named defendant in the proceedings has become the 'landlord' (as defined by section 44 of the 1954 Act) but has not been made a party by the time the matter has come on for trial, the court should usually adjourn the matter to allow an application for the new landlord to be joined or substituted as a party.

Meah v Sector Properties Ltd (1974)

In order to be valid, an application must be made by a person entitled to make it. An application for a new tenancy was struck out on the basis that the tenant has ceased to be the tenant of the property and had no standing under section 24(1) of the 1954 Act to apply for a new tenancy.

Williams v Hillcroft Garages (1971)

Failure to comply the required particulars in the application did not render it a nullity so as to justify it being struck out.

6.5 APPLICATION TO FIX TERMS OF A NEW TENANCY

The landlord can either oppose the grant of a new tenancy on the grounds specified in section 30(1) of the 1954 Act (see Chapter 7) or the terms of the new tenancy proposed by the tenant, or both. By section 29A, if the landlord does not oppose the grant of a new tenancy or fails to establish any of the grounds of opposition on which he is entitled to rely, then the court must order the grant of a new tenancy.

Morgan v Jones (1960)

Where parties have not agreed them in writing, the terms of the new tenancy must be determined by the court. The court should consider evidence as to the reasonableness of the terms. Failure by the landlord in the pleadings to expressly oppose the tenant's proposed terms does not mean that he necessarily agrees with them and should not prevent him from calling evidence as to whether they are reasonable.

Where the grant of a new tenancy is not opposed, a modified form of the Part 8 procedure should be used. The claim form should be served two months after the date of issue and the court will give directions about the future case management of the claim following receipt of the acknowledgment of service.

6.6   INITIAL CASE MANAGEMENT

6.6.1 General

The court's main function is to resolve issues raised on applications by tenants for new tenancies.

- Parties should identify the issues that need to be resolved at an early stage.
- If the parties are disputing both whether a tenancy should be granted and what the terms of such a tenancy should be, the grounds of opposition will normally be tried as a preliminary issue (CPR 56.PD.7H).
- If the landlord succeeds in making out his ground of opposition then the application for a new tenancy will be dismissed and no time and expense will have been taken up in adducing expert evidence on valuation and rent which in the event has proved irrelevant.
- If a new tenancy is ordered then the question of the rent and other terms can be decided at a further hearing if not agreed between the parties.
- Others points of law, such as the validity of the notices or whether the tenancy is one to which the 1954 Act applies, should usually also be decided as preliminary issues.
- If preliminary points are raised later. the claim would need to be amended or an application brought under CPR 23.

6.6.2 Directions and evidence

To enable the court to give directions, evidence supporting the parties' respective positions must be filed. Where the claim is opposed, evidence (including expert evidence) must be filed by the parties as the court directs. The landlord will be required to file his evidence first (CPR 56.PD.7F).

Directions about the future management of the claim will be given at the expiry of the time for service of the tenant's evidence, whether or not such evidence has been served. These are likely to include directions as to disclosure, expert evidence, site view (the court may be assisted by a view of the premises this should be raised with the judge at an early stage).

6.6.3 **Experts**

As the expert's first duty is to the court (see below at 8.2), he has a direct right of access to the court without the need to notify the parties and may file a written request for directions to assist him to carry out his functions as an expert (CPR 35.14).

Expert advisers have a professional duty to abide by timetables imposed by the courts.

- The court may specify a sanction for non-compliance with directions (which may include striking out a claim) (CPR 3.4(2)(c)).
- Where the court specifies a sanction for non-compliance with a direction by a set date, the parties may not extend that date by agreement (CPR 3.8(3)).
- In the event of non-compliance, the party in question must apply for relief from sanction under CPR 3.9.
- Where no sanction is imposed, an application can be made to impose a sanction for non-compliance under CPR 23.

7
Opposing the grant of a new tenancy

If the landlord establishes any of the grounds of opposition on which he is entitled to rely to the satisfaction of the court, the court must dismiss the application and not order the grant of a new tenancy (section 31 of the *Landlord and Tenant Act* 1954 ('1954 Act')). To this extent there is no element of discretion, although certain of the grounds of opposition do give the court a discretion.

7.1 NECESSARY CONTENTS OF THE SECTION 25 NOTICE

The landlord may terminate a tenancy (to which the 1954 Act applies) by serving a section 25 notice on the tenant. Such a notice must specify the date on which the tenancy is to end. It must also be in the prescribed form. The prescribed forms cover a number of essential matters and contain extensive explanatory notes for the guidance of tenants receiving a notice.

There are now two prescribed forms of section 25 notice: one for unopposed renewals and one for opposed renewals (as at the date of print, Forms 1 and 2 of Schedule 2 to the *Landlord and Tenant Act 1954, Part 2 (Notices) Regulations 2004*, respectively).

The timing, content and service of section 25 notices are considered in more detail in 4.1 above.

In order to be valid, a section 25 notice must:

- be served by the correct landlord;
- state whether the landlord is opposed to the grant of a new tenancy to the tenant; and

- if so, specify the grounds of opposition relied on under section 30(1);
- if not, set out the landlord's proposals as to:
  - the property to be comprised in the new tenancy;
  - the rent to be payable under the new tenancy; and
  - the other terms of the new tenancy.

A notice served by someone other than the landlord within the meaning of section 44 will not be valid.

Pearson v Alyo (1990)

The notice purporting to be given under section 25 stated only the name of the husband, who was the sole beneficial owner, although he and his wife were registered at the Land Registry as joint proprietors with title absolute. The court of Appeal were in no doubt that the notice was invalid. Nourse LJ said 'the Act would be unworkable' if it had regard to equitable owners.

Morrow v Nadeem (1986)

The Court of Appeal held that a section 25 notice served in the name, not of the landlord but of the majority shareholder in the landlord company, was bad.

Yamaha-Kemble Music (UK) Ltd v ARC Properties Ltd (1990)

The section 25 notice named ARC Properties Ltd as the landlord, when it was, however, the parent company, ARC Property Developments Ltd.

Minor drafting indiscretions may be saved by the *Landlord and Tenant Act 1954, Part II (Notices) Regulations* 1983. Under regulation 2(2), a notice is valid if it is in the prescribed form, or 'in ... a form substantially to the like effect'. The scope of this argument is not great, as only minor drafting indiscretions can thus be saved.

(See also *Bridgers v Sandford* (1991).)

Morrow v Nadeem (1986)

An argument based on these saving words to validate a notice naming the principal shareholder in the landlord company, not the landlord, failed. Nicholls LJ said:

> 'A form made out in such a way as not to give the real substance of the information required is not a form substantially to the like effect as the statutory form of notice.'

Barclays Bank plc v Bee (2001)

A notice expressing the landlord's intention to oppose the grant of a new tenancy, but failing to include any ground of opposition, is invalid.

Bridgers v Sandford (1991)

A notice not in the prescribed form was valid despite not complying precisely with the words of the 1954 Act because it fulfilled the purpose of the Act, which was to tell the landlord whether or not the tenant intended to oppose the notice.

Herongrove Ltd v Wates City of London Properties plc (1988)

A section 25 notice described the demised premises solely as office accommodation on the ninth floor of the demised premises, whereas under the lease, the demise included storage space on the lower ground and basement floors, and car parking spaces. Harman J held that an objective test was appropriate in deciding whether the notice could be saved, i.e. 'is the notice quite clear to a reasonable tenant reading it?' Applying that test, Harman J found that the notice was defective and void.

Philpson-Stow v Trevor Square (1981)

A notice specifying an intended ground of opposition using a different from of words from those in section 30(1) of the 1954 Act was valid.

[**Note:** The new prescribed form simply requires the relevant paragraph of section 30(1) to be specified.]

Lewis v MTC Cars (1975)

A notice in which the landlord had included a ground of opposition under section 30(1) of the 1954 Act but failed to delete the sentence in the prescribed form stating that he would not oppose the grant of a new tenancy was valid because the inclusion of the ground of opposition made it clear that the landlord intended to oppose the grant of a new tenancy.

7.2 DETERMINATION AS A PRELIMINARY ISSUE

The court will decide whether the landlord's grounds of opposition have been made out before considering the terms of the new tenancy.

Dutch Oven Ltd v Egham Estates and Investment Co Ltd (1968)

When the tenant's application for a new tenancy is opposed it will normally be convenient to try the ground of opposition first, possibly as a preliminary issue, and to stay all other issues, such as the terms of the new tenancy, to be determined at a subsequent hearing, if necessary:

- if the landlord succeeds, there is no longer any need to consider the terms of the new tenancy;
- if the landlord fails, the matter can be adjourned for the parties to prepare their cases on the terms of the new tenancy.

7.3 THE GROUNDS OF OPPOSITION

There are seven grounds of opposition in section 30(1) of the 1954 Act, they can be summarised as follows:

- *Ground (a)* – the tenant ought not to be granted a new tenancy in view of its failure to comply with its repairing obligations;
- *Ground (b)* – a new tenancy ought not to be granted in view of the tenant's persistent delay in paying rent;

- *Ground (c)* – a new tenancy ought not to be granted in view of other substantial breaches of the tenant's obligations or for a reason connected with the tenant's use or management of the holding;
- *Ground (d)* – the landlord has offered reasonable alternative accommodation;
- *Ground (e)* – where possession is required for letting or otherwise disposing of the property as a whole and the current tenancy is a subletting of part;
- *Ground (f)* – that on the termination of the current tenancy the landlord intends to demolish or reconstruct the premises comprised in the holding or a substantial part or to carry out substantial works of construction; and
- *Ground (g)* – the landlord intends to occupy the holding.

Grounds (a) to (c) all involve some default by the tenant. No fault on the part of the tenant is necessary in the other cases. Grounds (a) to (c) and (e) are the grounds which give the court discretion on whether to order the grant of a new tenancy, even when the landlord has made out his ground. In the other cases, the court has to refuse to order a new tenancy if the ground of opposition is made out to its satisfaction.

Betty's Cafés Ltd v Phillips Furnishing Stores Ltd (1959)

The date on which the facts underlying grounds (a) to (c) will need to be established is the date of the hearing.

Desbroderie Ltd v Segalov (1956)

The onus is on the landlord to establish the grounds which have been specified. He cannot rely on a ground which has not been specified in the section 25 notice or counter-notice to the tenant's section 26 request.

The consequences of specifying the wrong or insufficient grounds can be far reaching. This limitation extends to a landlord's successor in title who is prevented from relying on grounds which have not been specified in the notice given by his predecessor in title.

Nursey v P Currie (Dartford) Ltd (1959)

On the facts, the landlord was in a position to establish ground (f) but not ground (g). The only ground of opposition which he had specified was ground (g). Despite being able to establish it, he was not entitled to rely on ground (f) because it had not been specified as a ground of opposition. As a result he was unsuccessful in opposing the grant of a new tenancy.

Hutchinson v Lamberth (1984)

The Court of Appeal held that the County Court judge had no jurisdiction to allow an amendment to allow the landlord to rely on a ground of opposition which he had failed to specify in his section 25 notice.

In view of the above, a landlord might therefore be tempted to include in his section 25 notice a ground on which he does not really intend to rely or one which he anticipates may be required by a predecessor in title. However, the landlord must have an honest belief in the ground stated.

Betty's Cafés Ltd v Philips Furnishing Stores Ltd (1959)

Statements given in a notice must be given honestly and truthfully because the recipient of the notice must act according to its contents. A dishonest notice would be voidable and liable to be set aside for fraudulent misrepresentation.

Marks v British Waterways Board (1963)

A notice must not be deceptive or misleading but must be given in good faith.

Stroadbroke v Mitchell (1991)

A notice which contains a statement of the landlord's intention, which was false and made fraudulently by the giver of the notice, is invalid and of no effect.

7.3.1 **Ground (a) – failure to repair**

Section 30(1)(a) entitles a landlord to oppose an application for a new tenancy:

> '(a) where under the current tenancy the tenant has any obligations as respects the repair and maintenance of the holding, that the tenant ought not to be granted a new tenancy in view of the state of repair of the holding, being a state resulting from the tenant's failure to comply with the said obligations'.

Crown copyright material is reproduced with the permission of the Controller of HMSO and the Queen's Printer for Scotland.

The basic facts, which must be established under ground (a) are:

- the tenant must have an obligation in respect of the repair and maintenance of the holding;
- the holding is in a less than satisfactory state of repair as a result of the tenant's failure to comply with his obligation.

The landlord will wish to have evidence that there are substantial breaches of repairing covenant before the date on which he serves his notice. There should at least have been an inspection by a surveyor and an interim schedule of dilapidations prepared.

The tenant will normally appoint his own surveyor and the experts will meet to identify the areas in which they are in agreement and to clarify their points of disagreement. In some (but not all) cases the experts may wish to set out their respective contentions in a schedule prepared in official referee's form (a Scott Schedule).

Betty's Cafés Ltd v Phillips Furnishing Stores Ltd (1959)

The Court of Appeal held that the judge, when considering whether ground (a) was established, was not confined to considering the state of the holding as at the date of the section 25 notice but should take into account the state of repair or disrepair of the holding as at the date the case before him to be decided.

Once the basic facts under ground (a) have been established, the court has discretion as to whether or not it should refuse a new tenancy.

Lyons v Central Commercial Properties Ltd (1958)

The majority of the Court of Appeal (Harman J dissenting) held that the discretion was a wide one and that the court could take account of all relevant circumstances, including what is likely to happen if a new tenancy is granted.

Eichner v Midland Bank Executor and Trustee Co Ltd (1970)

Once the court has established facts as regards the tenant's past behaviour and performance, the court is entitled to consider all the circumstances in connection with the breach of covenant and the conduct of the tenant as a whole in regard to his obligations under the tenancy. The first instance judge (whose decision was upheld by the Court of Appeal) said:

> 'It must be considered very carefully whether it is fair to saddle the landlord with a tenant with whom he is in constant litigation'.

On that basis, a landlord is likely to be in a stronger position under ground (a) than when faced with an application for relief from forfeiture based on breach of repairing covenant. This is because, instead of simply asking the court to continue the term freely granted, the landlord would be forced to grant a new term to a tenant who has already been in breach.

Beard v Williams (1986)

In exercising its discretion, the court should ask itself whether the landlord's interest is likely to be prejudiced by the occurrence of the matters relied on as constituting reasons within section 30(1) of the 1954 Act.

The following information is likely to be relevant to the exercise of the court's discretion:

- the nature of the dilapidations;
- the length of time during which the dilapidations have existed;

- when the dilapidations were first brought to the tenant's attention;
- the significance and extent of the dilapidations;
- the effect of the dilapidations on the landlord's reversion;
- the reasons for any breach of covenant.

In order to persuade a court to exercise its discretion in his favour, a tenant may decide to comply with a schedule of dilapidations by the date of the hearing or offer an undertaking to carry out the works by a specified date. More weight is likely to be given to the undertaking if the tenant is in a position to give an undertaking as to when the works will be carried out and satisfy the court that he has sufficient funds.

Nihad v Chair (1956)

The tenant admitted being in breach of covenant to repair but was granted a new tenancy having regard to his willingness that the new lease should contain a repairing covenant and a proviso for re-entry, together with a covenant requiring the tenant to make good the breach by putting the premise forthwith into repair in accordance with the terms of the repairing covenants in the previous lease.

Lyons v Central Commercial Properties Ltd (1958)

The court refused to grant the tenant a new tenancy despite him giving an undertaking to carry out all works of repair for which he was liable under his underlease. The court took into account the fact that the tenant had had nearly a year to remedy the breaches but did not do so, that there were severe breaches, and that the tenant was not a small man likely to lose his livelihood, therefore not the sort of person who should be given relief.

Eichner v Midland Bank Executor and Trustee Co Ltd (1970)

The landlord opposed grant of new tenancy on grounds (a) and (c) (breach of other term of tenancy). Although the tenant had remedied the dilapidations by the date of the hearing, the court still refused to grant new tenancy, in view of a serious subsisting breach of user clause, the tenant's history of paying rent, his ability to pay rent in the future, and the unhappy landlord and tenant relationship over the years.

7.3.2 Ground (b) – persistent arrears

Section 30(1)(b) entitles a landlord to oppose an application for a new tenancy on the basis:

> '(b) that the tenant ought not to be granted a new tenancy in view of his persistent delay in paying rent which has become due'.

Crown copyright material is reproduced with the permission of the Controller of HMSO and the Queen's Printer for Scotland.

The basic requirements under ground (b) are:

- that there has been 'persistent delay' – establishing a long history of arrears will probably suffice; and
- that rent has 'become due' – this probably extends to all sums reserved as rent.

Escalus Properties Ltd v Robinson (1996)

The words in the respective leases, stating that the service charge was additional rent and recoverable as rent, gave to the service charge the character and attributes of rent.

To demonstrate the rental arrears, the landlord should prepare a schedule of arrears, showing:

- the rent which has become due under the terms of the tenancy and the amount;
- the payments which have been made by the tenant and the length of the delay;
- the total rent which from time to time has been due and unpaid;
- the reminders which have been sent and the form they took; and
- the enforcement action, if any, which has been taken.

The schedule should, if possible, be agreed with the tenant. In the absence of agreement, the landlord will need to be in a position to prove the matters set out in the schedule (by documentary and oral evidence).

Once the basic facts under ground (b) have been established, the court has a discretion as to whether or not to grant a new tenancy. Each case is judged on its own facts.

Rawashdeh v Lane (1988)

The Court of Appeal will only interfere with the judge's exercise of his discretion if it is apparent that he has made an error of principle, if he exercised his discretion in a way which was patently perverse, or if he took into account an irrelevant factor or failed to take into account a relevant factor.

Hurstfell Ltd v Leicester Square Property Co Ltd (1988)

The onus is on the landlord to persuade the court not to grant a new tenancy. However, the tenant is obliged to explain the reasons for the past failures and to satisfy the court that if a new lease were granted, the rent would be paid on time. On the facts, the judge was satisfied with the tenant's explanation of the past failures (tenant had bought a bankrupt plastic toy enterprise from a company in liquidation) and was also satisfied that there would be no recurrence. Although there was less evidence to support the latter conclusion and financial evidence arguably pointing to the contrary, the Court of Appeal refused to interfere with the judge's findings.

The following are likely to be relevant to the exercise of the court's discretion:

- The trouble, time and expense the tenant's default has caused the landlord. [The landlord should provide details of managing agent's time, administrative time, legal expenses, etc.]
- Whether or not the landlord had objected to the tenant's delay.
- Any excuse or explanation by the tenant for the delay in making payment.
- The tenant's financial resources and the likelihood of the obligations being met in the future.

- Any offer by the tenant to pay rent in advance or to give security. [This will often (but not always) persuade a court to give a tenant a second chance.]
- Whether the rent is so far in arrears as to give the landlord a right to forfeit.
- Whether the landlord has actually taken forfeiture proceedings.

Hopcutt v Carver (1969)

The County Court judge dismissed the application for a new tenancy on the grounds that the tenant had persistently delayed paying his rent. The Court of Appeal refused to interfere with the judge's discretion on the basis that there was evidence on which the judge had based his conclusions and he had made no error of principle.

Horowitz v Ferrand (1956)

A landlord is not to be expected to be required to chase a tenant for his rent and it is not necessary under ground (b) for the arrears to be substantial or last for a long period of time. On the facts, although the tenant's rent was always paid, it was usually paid late and only after the landlord had been forced to call for it. The court refused to grant a new tenancy.

Freeman v Barclays Bank Ltd (1958)

The tenant had been in persistent and substantial arrears for a period of five years before the hearing. The fact that the landlord had corresponded with the tenant for two years in that period without raising any complaint about the arrears did not prevent him from relying on ground (b) but was a matter to which the court could have regard in the exercise of its discretion. On the facts, the landlord was entitled to rely on ground (b).

Hazel v Hassan Akhtar (2001)

Acquiescence by the landlord in the tenant's persistent failure to pay rent on time estopped both the landlord and his successor in title from relying on ground (b) unless reasonable notice was given to the tenant to revert to strict compliance with the terms of the lease. On the facts, there had been repeated minor breaches in the tenant's obligation under the lease to pay rent. A Schedule of Arrears prepared for March 1997 to December 2000 showed that rent was between one and 21 days in arrears for each quarter. Rent was paid by cheque and a period had been allowed for the rent to clear.

Hurstfell Ltd v Leicester Square Property Co Ltd (1988)

The court granted a new tenancy in circumstances where the tenant had a lamentable rent payment record which commenced two years after assignment of the lease. Under the lease, the rent was payable quarterly on the usual quarter days. In respect of each of the 11 quarter days from Lady Day 1984 to Christmas Day 1986, the tenant was late with its rent payments: on one occasion payment was no less than 19 weeks late; on another 17 weeks; on three other occasions it was nine or ten weeks late; and on the other occasions the delay was four, five or six weeks. In addition to late payments of rent, there were comparable delays in paying sums due for insurance. The landlord inevitably had to chase the tenant constantly for payment. Cheques sent by the tenant to the landlord were dishonoured. Promises were not fulfilled. On two occasions, the landlord started proceedings for payment of the rent, and the landlord incurred costs in seeking to get the money due to it. The Court of Appeal refused to interfere with the first instance judge's decision.

[See also *Rawashdeh v Lane* (1988) above.]

7.3.3 Ground (c) – other breaches or reasons

Section 30(1)(c) entitles a landlord to oppose an application for a new tenancy on the basis:

> '(c) that the tenant ought not to be granted a new tenancy in view of other substantial breaches by him of his obligations under the current tenancy, or for any other reason connected with the tenant's use or management of the holding'.

Crown copyright material is reproduced with the permission of the Controller of HMSO and the Queen's Printer for Scotland.

The ambit of this ground of opposition is extremely wide. It has two limbs:

- 'other substantial breaches' of covenant not falling within grounds (a) and (b); or
- 'other reasons' connected with the tenant's use or management of the holding not falling within the first limb and grounds (a) and (b).

Where the landlord is relying on other breaches, he will need to prove them to the satisfaction of the court in the usual way. Unlike under grounds (a) and (b), the 'other breaches' under the first limb are not confined to breaches affecting the holding.

Jones v Jenkins (1986)

Use of three rooms as a laundry and massage parlour in breach of the tenancy obligations (which required them to be used as an annexe to a 'nature cure centre') may well constitute an 'other substantial breach' so as to bring the landlord within ground (c).

Jones v Christy (1963)

The lease provided for premises not to be used other than as a private residence for the profession of a veterinary surgeon and granted fishing rights over a stretch of river. The tenant did not use the premises as such but let the fishing rights and used a room in the premises as a drying room. The landlord was entitled to rely on the first limb of ground (c).

The 'other reasons' under the second limb of ground (c) are matters which are not covered by grounds (a) or (b) or the first limb of ground (c). Although this limb is very wide, the other reasons must be connected with the use and management of the holding. For example, this may require the landlord to show that the tenant's use or management of the holding is illegal or immoral or contrary to planning policy.

Cheryl Investments v Saldanha; Royal Life Saving Society v Page (1978)

Lord Denning suggested that a tenant lawfully altered the nature of his tenancy by changing his user, so that it ceased to be Rent Act protected and fell within the protection of the 1954 Act might be exposed to a successful application by the landlord under ground (c) on the ground that he has surreptitiously, without the consent of the landlord, changed the use of the holding.

Turner and Bell v Searles (Stanford-le-Hope) Ltd (1977)

In considering the second limb of ground (c), the court is entitled to look at everything which it considers relevant in connection with the tenant's past, present and future use or management of the holding which might enable it to fairly exercise its discretion. On the facts, the tenant's continued use of the premises had become a criminal offence under section 89(5) of the *Town and Country Planning Act* 1971 [see now, section 179 of the *Town and Country Planning Act* 1990] and the tenant intended to carry on the illegal use if granted a new tenancy. The grant of a new tenancy would have sanctioned the unlawful character of the use of the premises.

Beard v Williams (1986)

The precarious nature of the tenant's living arrangements constituted a 'reason' connected with the tenant's use or management of the holding within ground (c). On the facts, the tenant carried on the business of breeding greyhounds and resided in a van stationed unlawfully some 100 yards from the kennels. The satisfactory continuation of his breeding activities depended on the tenant's ability to continue to reside sufficiently close to the kennels. If his business suffered, the landlord would be prejudiced.

Once the basic facts under (c) have been established, the court has a discretion as to whether or not to grant a new tenancy. The discretion is exercised on the same basis as under grounds (a) and (b), above.

The following factors are likely to be relevant to the exercise of the court's discretion:

- whether the landlord has complained about the breaches during the current tenancy; and
- if so, what action the tenant has taken to remedy them;
- the trouble, time and expense past breaches have caused the landlord;
- any excuse or explanation by the tenant for past breaches;
- any undertaking by the tenant to do something positive for the future;
- whether the breaches or matters relied on are technical or whether they have caused loss and inconvenience to the public at large.

7.3.4 Ground (d) – suitable alternative accommodation

Section 30(1)(d) entitles the landlord to oppose the grant of a new tenancy on the basis:

> '(d) that the landlord has offered and is willing to provide or secure the provision of alternative accommodation for the tenant, that the terms on which the alternative accommodation is available are reasonable having regard to the terms of the current tenancy and to all other relevant circumstances, and that the accommodation and the time at which it will be available are suitable for the tenant's requirements (including the requirement to preserve goodwill) having regard to the nature and class of his business and to the situation and extent of, and facilities afforded by, the holding'.

Crown copyright material is reproduced with the permission of the Controller of HMSO and the Queen's Printer for Scotland.

The basic requirements under ground (d) are that:

- there must be an 'offer' by landlord to provide or secure alternative accommodation;
- the offer must be reasonable (having regard to the terms of the tenancy and other relevant circumstances);
- the offer must contain sufficient detail so as to be capable of acceptance;
- the accommodation itself must be suitable for the tenant's requirements (having regard to the nature and class of his

business and to the situation and extent of, and facilities *afforded by the building)*;

- the time at which the accommodation is available must be suitable for the tenants requirements;
- the landlord must be 'willing' to provide or secure the accommodation for the tenant – the willingness must be tested at the date of the hearing.

M Chaplin Ltd v Regent Capital Holdings Ltd (1994)

The requirement in ground (d) that the landlord has offered alternative accommodation is satisfied by an offer of accommodation before the issue is joined in the pleadings, namely before the landlord files his answer in the County Court or his affidavit in reply in the High Court. On the facts, an offer of alternative accommodation was made in the letter under cover of which the section 25 notice was served. This was held to comply with the requirements of section 30(1)(d).

Betty's Cafés Ltd v Phillips Furnishing Stores Ltd (1959)

Viscount Simonds stated that it would not be reasonable to reduce the time within which the landlord should have the opportunity of finding and offering alternative accommodation. This suggests that if the accommodation offered by the landlord has become unavailable, the landlord can use the time up until the hearing to find other suitable alternative accommodation and to revise his offer accordingly.

O'May v City of London Real Property Co Ltd (1983)

In determining reasonableness of the offer, the court must begin by considering the terms of the current tenancy. The onus of persuading the court to impose a change against the will of another rests on the party proposing the change. The change must be fair and reasonable taking into account, amongst other things, the comparatively weak negotiating position of a sitting tenant requiring renewal, particularly in conditions of scarcity, and the general purpose of the 1954 Act, namely the protection of the business interests of the tenant.

To assist the court in deciding the question of suitability, it may be convenient to put before the court a location plan and for oral evidence to be given by an expert to enable the court to compare the nature, location, physical dimensions and layout of the proposed accommodation with those of the current premises. In judging suitability, the court should have regard to the following factors:

- the nature and class of the tenant's business and whether the accommodation is suited to it;
- the situation and extent of the holding; and
- the facilities afforded by the holding.

M Chaplin Ltd v Regent Capital Holdings Ltd (1994)

The alternative accommodation does not have to mirror exactly the existing accommodation. Accommodation on the second floor was suitable as an alternative to existing ground floor accommodation.

Betty's Cafés Ltd v Phillips Furnishing Stores Ltd (1959)

Unlike the previous grounds, once the relevant matters have been established, the court *must* grant a new tenancy: there is no discretion. No compensation is payable (see Chapter 10).

7.3.5 Ground (e) – tenancy created by subletting of part of the property

Section 30(1)(e) entitles the landlord to oppose the grant of a new tenancy:

> '(e) where the current tenancy was created by the sub-letting of part only of the property comprised in a superior tenancy and the landlord is the owner of an interest in reversion expectant on the termination of that superior tenancy, that the aggregate of the rents reasonably obtainable on separate lettings of the holding and the remainder of that property would be substantially less than the rent reasonably obtainable on a letting of that

property as a whole, that on the termination of the current tenancy the landlord requires possession of the holding for the purpose of letting or otherwise disposing of the said property as a whole, and that in view thereof the tenant ought not to be granted a new tenancy'.

Crown copyright material is reproduced with the permission of the Controller of HMSO and the Queen's Printer for Scotland.

This ground would entitle a landlord to recover possession of part of premises that have been sublet to enable him to let or otherwise dispose of the whole.

The conditions which must be satisfied under ground (e) are:

- the current tenancy must have been created by a subletting of part only of premises comprised in a superior tenancy;
- the landlord must show that on termination of the current tenancy he requires possession of the holding for the purpose of letting or otherwise disposing of the property as a whole – the landlord must prove both his intention for the premises and his ability to implement that intention (see 7.3.6);
- the 'landlord' must be the superior landlord at the date on which he gives his notice;
- a valuation exercise must be carried out in order to determine whether the rents achievable on separate lettings would be 'substantially less' than a letting of the whole.

The landlord will require valuation evidence. In the absence of valuation evidence, the landlord will be unable to prove his case under ground (e).

The valuation evidence should state the rent that could be obtained at the date of the hearing:

- on a separate letting of the holding comprised in the subtenancy;
- on a separate letting of the rest of the property comprised in the superior tenancy;
- on a letting of the whole.

It is for the valuer to advise (and justify) what evidence appears to him to be appropriate in order to substantiate his opinion on rent.

Civil Procedure Rules 1998 ('CPR'), Rule 35.5

Expert evidence is to be given in a written report unless the court directs otherwise. For the form and contents of experts' reports, see CPR 35.10 and *Practice Direction (Experts and Assessors)*, paragraphs 1.1 to 1.6 (35.PD.1).

Ideally, the valuer's report should be set out along the following lines:

- The identity, qualifications and relevant experience of the valuer.
- The relevant facts. These can be briefly summarised with more detail set out in an appendix.
- The valuer's instructions, including the valuation date and any assumptions made.
- The property, including measurements and whether these are agreed.
- The area in which the property is situated, so far as is relevant to the valuation.
- The terms under which the property is held. These can be briefly summarised with the detail in an appendix.
- The evidence relied on. This should refer to an appendix listing the documents read and giving detail of the inspections made of the property and of the comparables and any research done by the valuer, i.e. talking to local agents.
- The comparables. Wherever possible these should be evidenced by signed pro formas. If not, the valuer should state the source of his information. The key details are best contained in the report, rather than an appendix.
- The market. An account of the supply of and demand for of properties of this kind around the valuation date.
- Adjustments needed to the comparables.
- Analysis. This is the most important section. The valuer should explain which comparables are best and why and discuss the adjustments made in the case of each.
- The valuation.
- Declaration of honesty and independence as required by RICS and CPR.
- List of appendices.

The duties of the valuer as an expert witness are considered in 9.2 below.

Once the basic facts under ground (e) have been established, the court has a discretion as to whether or not to grant a new tenancy. Compensation is payable (see Chapter 10).

Greaves Organisation v Stanhope Gate Property Co (1973)

Surrender of superior tenancy before service of section 25 notice precluded landlord from relying on ground (e).

Palset v Grinling (1948)

'Substantial' means not only de minimis but 'great, weighty, big or solid'.

The latter requirement means that the landlord will need to show his ability to obtain vacant possession of other premises not comprised in the holding – if the superior tenancy is one to which the Act applies, he will need to be able to show that he can determine it.

7.3.6 Ground (f) – demolition and reconstruction

Section 30(1)(f) entitles a landlord to oppose the grant of a new tenancy on the basis:

> '(f) that on the termination of the current tenancy the landlord intends to demolish or reconstruct the premises comprised in the holding or a substantial part of those premises or to carry out substantial work of construction on the holding or part thereof and that he could not reasonably do so without obtaining possession of the holding'.

Crown copyright material is reproduced with the permission of the Controller of HMSO and the Queen's Printer for Scotland.

The basic requirements under ground (f) are that:

- the relevant date at which the various aspects of the proposal are to be considered is on the termination of the current tenancy;

- the person who must have the relevant intention is *the landlord*;
- the landlord must have the necessary *intention*;
- the intention must be either to:

  - demolish or reconstruct the premises comprised in the holding, or
  - demolish or reconstruct ... a substantial part of those premises, or
  - to carry out substantial work of construction on the holding, or
  - to carry out substantial work of construction on ... part thereof; and

- the landlord *could not reasonably do so without obtaining possession of the holding.*

7.3.6.1 Necessary works

Ground (f) contains two limbs, namely whether the landlord intends to:

(i) demolish or reconstruct the premises comprised in the holding, or a substantial part of those premises, and
(ii) carry out works of construction on the holding or part thereof.

The correct way to approach the first limb is to identify the components in the proposed works that in some way affect the structure of the building, either internally or externally and to consider them in conjunction with any ancillary works that do not affect the structure.

Global Grange Ltd v Marazzi (2003)

On the facts, proposed works aimed at upgrading a hotel from a two-star to a four-star establishment did not satisfy the requirements of ground (f). The proposed works compromised the removal of stud partition walls, sub-division of rooms and installation of new rooms to create en suite facilities. The judge held that the works did not amount to reconstruction within the first limb of ground (f) and did not amount to substantial work of construction within the second limb of ground (f).

The Court of Appeal refused to interfere with the judge's decision, holding that the decision on ground (f) is a decision in the nature of an evaluation with which the appellate court should be slow to interfere.

[See also *IvoryGrove Ltd v Global Grange Ltd* (2003).]

Biles v Caeser (1957)

A landlord seeking to rely on ground (f) is not limited to the specific works, which he has specified in his section 25 notice, but may prove an intention to carry out the various kinds of work referred to under that ground.

The landlord must establish that his works comprise one of the following:

- demolition of the premises comprised in the holding;
- demolition of a substantial part of the premises comprised in the holding;
- reconstruction of the premises comprised in the holding;
- reconstruction of a substantial part of the premises comprised in the holding;
- substantial work of construction on the holding; or
- substantial work of construction on part of the premises comprised in the holding.

Housleys Ltd v Bloomer-Holt Ltd (1966)

The 'premises' are those parts of the holding which are capable of being demolished and reconstructed. Where the landlord intended to demolish a wooden garage covering about one-third of the site and the brick boundary wall, this was sufficient. The court also held that laying down a sufficient area of concrete can amount to substantial work of construction.

Turner v Wandsworth London Borough Council (1994)

A proposal to dig up old hard standing on a strip of land near to some railway lines, demolish the buildings on the site, lay tarmacadam or concrete on part and arrange for the rest to be planted with grass and trees was work of 'demolition' of the premises comprised in the holding.

Percy E Cadle & Co Ltd v Jacmarch Properties Ltd (1957)

'Reconstruction' means a substantial interference with the structure of the premises and then a rebuilding in probably a different form.

Cook v Mott (1961)

'Construction' includes new or additional work: 'it would be difficult to reconstruct something unless first of all there was a construction which was wholly or partly demolished'.

Romulus Trading Co Ltd v Trustees of Henry Smith's Charity (1990)

For works, they should involve the structure of the building but structure is not confined to the exterior or load bearing walls. Works which are preparatory and works ancillary to or 'closely associated with' the qualifying works.

Barth v Prichard (1990)

The refurbishment or improvement of the interior by rewiring the electricity supply, installing partitions as well as new central heating and re-siting the toilets does not amount to substantial work of construction. Some form of building upon the premises involving the structure is required.

Joel v Swaddle (1957)

The court emphasised that the work must be to the holding. The effect of the work as a whole as opposed to each item individually should be taken into account to determine whether the work is sufficient to constitute reconstruction.

Atkinson v Bettison (1955)

Whether there is a 'substantial' work of construction is a question of fact and degree looking at totality of the works. One of the meanings of 'substantial' is 'considerable, solid or big'.

7.3.6.2 The landlord's intention

The landlord's intention must be able to do the necessary works on the termination of the current tenancy which has been held to mean a reasonable time from the date of its termination (see *Method Development v Jones* (1971)).

Live Stock Underwriting Agency v Corbett and Newson (1955)

What constitutes a reasonable time is a question of fact. On the facts, work was to start within three months after the termination of a tenancy. This was held to be sufficient.

Cunliffe v Goodman (1950)

A provisional desire is not enough. The landlord must have made a definite decision as well as having a reasonable prospect of being able to implement that decision without there being too many hurdles to overcome. 'Intention' will not be proved, if the person professing it has too many hurdles to overcome, or has little control of events.

The court held that the project must have 'moved out of the zone of contemplation – out of the sphere of the tentative, the provisional and exploratory – into the valley of decision'.

Betty's Cafés Ltd v Phillips Furnishing Stores Ltd (1957)

The landlord's motives are irrelevant if he can show that he has the necessary intention. This is so even if the motive is simply a desire to get rid of the tenant. However, the landlord's primary purpose may be relevant in trying to decide whether the intention expressed is in fact genuine or merely colourable.

The intention must exist at the date of the hearing of the application but need not have existed when the section 25 notice was given.

Betty's Cafés Ltd v Phillips Furnishing Stores Ltd (1959)

Thus, where the landlord company passed a resolution regarding its intention to carry out the work during the hearing of the application, coupled with an authority to counsel to give an undertaking that the proposed works would be carried out as soon as practicable, this was held to be sufficient.

AD Wimbush & Son Ltd v Franmills Properties Ltd and others (1961)

As it is the competent landlord at the date of the hearing whose intention is relevant, he may rely on a notice given by a previous landlord.

7.3.6.3 Proof of intention/implementing desire

Where a landlord offers an undertaking to the court that he will carry out certain works, this will be powerful, though not conclusive, evidence of fixity of intention.

Betty's Cafés Ltd v Phillips Furnishing Stores Ltd (1959)

The court accepted an undertaking from the landlord to carry out the proposed works.

London Hilton Jewellers Ltd v Hilton International Hotels Ltd (1990)

A landlord's undertaking to carry out alterations to the holding so as to enlarge the hotel bar confirmed 'fixity of intention'.

Chez Gerard v Greene (1983)

An undertaking was offered in the course of counsel's closing.

If the competent landlord is an individual, his intention will probably have to be proved by giving evidence. Where the landlord is a company then intention is normally proved by board minutes. Steps taken towards implementing the necessary intention can assist the court in reaching the conclusion that the necessary intention has been formed. It also helps to show that there are not too many obstacles in the way of achieving the intention.

Reohorn v Barry Corporation (1956)

The landlord is not obliged to show that he will definitely be able to implement his intention but must show that there is a reasonable prospect that he will bring about what he intends.

The factors likely to be relevant to this question are:

- whether the premises are ripe for redevelopment;
- the existence of planning permission;
- the existence of working drawings and specifications;
- the existence of listed building consent, if applicable;
- mortgagees' consent if, this is required;
- the availability of finance;
- viability of the scheme;
- the preparation of tender documentation; and
- the solving of any rights of light problems.

These factors are not exhaustive and neither does the landlord have to prove that all of these or a majority of them are in place or have been dealt with. What he has to establish is that there is a reasonable prospect of being able to do what he intends.

Palisade Investments v Collin Estates (1992)

Balcombe LJ said that it is not always appropriate to test reasonable practicability by reference to the presence or absence of detailed building plans, planning and licensing consents.

Gregson v Cyril Lord (1963)

If the landlord does not have planning permission, the test is whether a reasonable man, on the evidence, would believe that the landlord had a reasonable prospect of getting that permission.

Reohorn v Barry Corporation (1956)

It will not be sufficient if he proposes to have the work done by way of an agreement for a building lease if the arrangements are purely tentative.

Dolgellau Golf Club v Hett (1998)

The function of the judicial gloss on the statutory test of intention is to determine the reality of a landlord's intention to start a business, not the probability of his achieving its start, or even less, its ultimate success.

Cadogan v McCarthy & Stone Developments (1996)

In assessing intention, the court is not to have regard to the wisdom or long-term viability of the project.

7.3.6.4 Requirement for possession of the holding

Not only must the landlord show an intention to carry out the qualifying works, he must also show that he could not reasonably do them without obtaining possession of the holding. What, in substance, this provision amounts to, is that the tenant can have a new tenancy if the landlord can carry out the work proposed around him.

Heath v Drown (1973)

Possession means legal possession and not physical possession. There must be a legal right for the landlord to do the works under the terms of the current tenancy in order for it to be found that he does not require 'possession'. Where the landlord has rights under the tenancy for entering and carrying out the proposed works, he was not able to show that legal possession was required and was irrelevant that the tenant would have been prevented from having access to the premises for his business whilst the works were in progress. As a result, he failed to establish the necessary intention under ground (f).

Price v Esso Petroleum Co (1980)

In a lease of premises enabling the landlord to enter to carry out improvements, it was held that this prevented the landlord from opposing the grant of a new tenancy because he did not require legal possession of the premises to carry out the demolition and reconstruction.

Graysim Holdings v P & O Property Holdings (1993)

Where carrying out the works without obtaining possession of the premises would have cost the landlord an additional £33,000, it was held to be unreasonable.

Landlord and Tenant Act 1954, section 31A

The tenant can defeat a landlord's opposition to the grant of a new tenancy if he agrees to the inclusion in the terms of a new tenancy of terms giving the landlord access and other facilities for carrying out the work intended and that, given that access and those facilities, the landlord could reasonably carry out the work without obtaining possession of the holding and without interfering to a substantial extent, or for a substantial time, with the use of the holding for the purposes of the business carried on by the tenant.

Decca Navigator Co v Greater London Council (1974)

The work which must be looked at is the work which the landlord actually intends to carry out. The court cannot enquire as to whether the extent of the works proposed is strictly necessary.

The works must be capable of reasonably being carried out without interfering, to a substantial extent or for a substantial time, with the use of the holding for the purposes of the tenant's business. What is relevant is the physical interference with the use of the holding for the purposes of the business. The effect that it will have on the tenant's business is irrelevant.

Redfern v Reeves (1979)

Where the works would have resulted in completely excluding the tenant from the holding for one to two months, this was held to constitute substantial interference.

Cerex Jewels v Peachy Property Corporation (1986)

Exclusion from the holding for two weeks was held to be insufficient interference.

Blackburn v Hussain (1988)

The qualifying work would have prevented trading for 12 weeks – it would be impossible for the tenant to run his café business and for that period the landlord would be required to use the whole of the café premises, although café equipment could be shifted from one room to another with removing it from the premises. The Court of Appeal (overruling the decision of the first instance judge) held that the nature of the interference for a period of 12 weeks was interference, to a substantial extent and for a substantial time, with the use of the café for the purpose of the business carried on by the tenant.

7.3.7 Ground (g) – landlord intends to occupy

Section 30(g) entitles a landlord to oppose an application for a new tenancy:

> '(g) subject as hereinafter provided, that on the termination of the current tenancy the landlord intends to occupy the holding for the purposes, or partly for the purposes, of a business to be carried on by him therein, or as his residence'.

Crown copyright material is reproduced with the permission of the Controller of HMSO and the Queen's Printer for Scotland.

The basic requirements under ground (g) are that:

- the landlord must have the requisite intention;
- the intention must be to occupy the holding;

- the occupation must be wholly or partly for business purposes or as his residence; and
- the business must be carried on by the landlord.

7.3.7.1 **Intention**

The qualities of the landlord's intention under ground (g) are the same as the qualities required under ground (f).

The landlord must prove that he has the practical possibility of carrying of his intention. The following factors likely to assist are:

- proof that he has given serious thought to the manner in which the business will be carried out and to its potential profitability;
- advice obtained as to the above;
- prior business experience;
- if the intention is for the business to be run through a manager, or to employ staff, evidence of any arrangements which have been made;
- evidence of other preparatory steps to the start up of the business, i.e. proposals for the acquisition of stock, obtaining estimates for shop fittings;
- if the proposal involves a change of business, evidence that no planning permission is required or that there is a reasonable prospect of it being obtained.

Cox v Binfield (1989)

The landlord had a need and a powerful wish to obtain the tenant's accommodation. His plans were ill-thought out and might well fail but were not so unrealistic as not to be genuine.

In some cases, a landlord has offered to the applicant and to the court an undertaking that he will occupy the premises for his own business upon getting possession. The offer of such an undertaking does not necessarily conclude the case; it has to be examined in the light of the circumstances in which it is offered and the evidence as to the capability of the person offering it to carry it out, and may be discounted.

Lennox v Bell (1957)

The landlord gave an undertaking that she would commence the business of a greengrocer 'as soon as practicable' if she obtained possession. The court found that, due to the landlord's ill health, it was unlikely that she would be able to carry on the business, despite her hopes that she would obtain assistance from close family. The undertaking, whilst not made in bad faith, was of little worth.

Lightcliffe and District Cricket and Lawn Tennis Club v Walton (1977)

The court ignored the landlord's undertaking that he would occupy the tenant's land for the purposes of grazing cattle on the basis that the land in question was of poor quality and would require considerable treatment before it would become suitable for grazing, which would involve considerable expenditure by the landlord.

The court held that an undertaking given by a substantial company of good reputation was likely to be more dependable than an undertaking given by an individual who for personal reasons may find it necessary or expedient to change his mind.

Chez Gerard v Greene (1983)

The judge held that the intention to run a restaurant business from the premises has been proved and concluded that he would find in favour of the landlord 'only if' the undertaking was given. The Court of Appeal held that the undertaking had been properly accepted as one of the factors which the judge had taken account for its evidential value in establishing intention.

Espresso Coffee Machine Co v Guardian Assurance Co (1959)

The landlord company relied on a board resolution to occupy the premises for business if possession was obtained. The landlord's counsel gave an undertaking in the terms of the resolution. It was held that the board resolution was an adequate indication of a fixed, settled and real intention and counsel's undertaking on behalf of the company acted to 'compel fixity of intention'.

Hunt v Decca Navigator Co (1972)

Where a landlord wished to regain possession of land for use as a car park adjoining its office building, the ground of opposition was made out. Using the car park for staff visiting the adjoining building was not use of a car park for a business carried on elsewhere, but was use of the car park for a business carried out on the site and elsewhere as well.

7.3.7.2 Occupation of the holding

Method Development v Jones (1971)

The carrying of a business in a substantial part of the holding will be sufficient.

If the landlord intends to demolish buildings which form part of the holding before going into occupation, he may not intend to occupy 'the holding'.

Nursey v P Currie (Dartford) Ltd (1959)

On the facts, the tenancy consisted of some small buildings in a yard and the landlord intended to demolish the buildings and turn the yard into a petrol filling station for his own occupation. The Court of Appeal held that the landlord failed to establish ground (g). Willmer LJ held that an intention to occupy the holding meant an intention to occupy the property described in the parcels clause in the lease and consequently if the landlord intended to destroy those parcels he could not be said to intend to occupy the holding.

Method Development v Jones (1971)

Intention to take occupation of part of the holding on the termination of the current tenancy and to use approximately four-fifths of it, but with a different partitioning layout, for landlord's business as from then or 12 months thereafter was enough for the purposes of ground (g).

Cam Gears v Cunningham (1981)

The tenant occupied a car park, and the landlord intended to incorporate the land in to his business of vehicle testing, and to erect upon it a workshop, offices and inspection pits. It was held that the 'holding' consisted of the vacant site and that this is what the landlord intended to occupy, even though he intended to erect buildings on it.

Leathwoods Ltd v Total Oil Great Britain Ltd (1985)

The tenant occupied a petrol filling station and the landlord intended to demolish and reconstruct it by building a new petrol filling station in order to occupy it. This was held to be 'intention to occupy' the holding and the landlord was entitled to rely on ground (g).

Thornton v Blacks Leisure Group (1986)

The tenant occupied a shop, and the landlords, who occupied the shop next door intended to remove walls separating the two shops and incorporate the two shops into one unit for their own occupation. The judge accepted that the landlords have established an intention within ground (g).

7.3.7.3 **Business carried on by the landlord**

Cafeteria (Keighley) v Harrison (1956)

The landlord need not have an intention to occupy the premises personally. It is sufficient if he intends to occupy and carry on his business through an agent or manager.

Chez Gerard v Greene (1983)

A Liberian shipping company with no experience of running a restaurant was able to establish an intention to run a restaurant under ground (g) through an agreement with an experienced restaurateur manager.

Skeet v Powell-Sheddon (1988)

Ground of opposition succeeded where the landlord proposed to operate a hotel by entering into a partnership with her husband who would be responsible for day-to-day management, with the prospect of her daughter, who was studying hotel management, becoming manageress in due course.

Parkes v Westminster Roman Catholic Diocese Trustee (1978)

Ground of opposition succeeded where parish priest was to occupy on behalf of the trustees of the diocese.

Pegler v Craven (1952)

Opposition under this ground will fail if, instead of the intended occupier being the agent of the landlord, the landlord is to occupy as agent for some other person – the landlord must fail under ground (g).

Landlord and Tenant Act 1954, section 30(3)

Where the landlord has a controlling interest in a company, any business to be carried on by the company is to be treated for the purposes of this paragraph as a business to be carried on by him.

Landlord and Tenant Act 1954, section 41(2)

Thus, where the landlord is a trustee, intended occupation by any of the beneficiaries under the trust will satisfy ground (g).

(See *Frish v Barclays Bank* (1955).)

Meyer v Riddick (1990)

However, the occupation must be as beneficiary under the trust. If, therefore, the trustees propose to enter into a commercial arrangement with one of the beneficiaries, or three trustees propose to enter into a lease to two of their number plus a stranger to the trust, that will not suffice.

7.3.7.4 **Five-year bar**

There is one very important limit set to the operation of ground (g) by section 30(2) of the 1954 Act. The landlord cannot rely on this ground of opposition if his interest was purchased or created in the five years prior to the termination of the current tenancy and the holding has been comprised in a tenancy or successive tenancies within the Act ever since his interest was purchased or created.

HL Bolton Engineering Co Ltd v TJ Graham and Sons (1957)

The object of the rule is that persons should not be able to purchase the reversions upon business tenancies just before they end and then obtain possession for their own purposes. Landlords who have acquired the reversion over the head of the sitting tenant, either by purchase or by the grant of a concurrent leasehold interest, within the five-year period are ruled out.

It was also held that the word 'purchased' is used in its popular sense of 'buying for money'.

Lawrence v Freeman Hardy & Willis (1959)

The five-year period is reckoned backwards from the date of termination of the tenant's current tenancy. The date of termination of the tenant's current tenancy is the date specified in the section 25 notice, or in the tenant's request for a new tenancy, ignoring the possible duration of interim continuation under section 64 of the 1954 Act.

It was also held that money is not confined to cash in its strict sense but excludes the acquisition of property in consideration for the giving of a covenant. The word 'purchased' does not include the surrender of an interest for no monetary consideration.

On the facts, where the landlord acquired the business of his predecessor in title together with certain freehold and leasehold properties, the fact that no part of the substantial consideration was apportioned to the leasehold reversion in question did not prevent it from being a 'purchase' for the purposes of the Act.

The court also held that the word 'created' is referable to the creation of the landlord's interest and not to the creation of the landlord's title.

Morar v Chauhan (1985)

A trustee landlord is not prevented from relying on ground (g) by the five-year bar by the creation of the trust or even if there has been a change in the identity of the trustee and beneficiaries during the five-year period.

Northcote Laundry v Donnelly (1968)

In the case of a leasehold interest, the interest is created when the lease is executed, and not at the date, if later, when the term is expressed to begin.

Denny Thorn & Co v George Harker & Co (1957)

Similarly, where the lease is registrable under the Land Registration Acts, the interest is created when the lease is granted, and not the later date when it is registered at HM Land Registry.

Cornish v Brook Green Laundry (1959)

Where the landlord has entered into an agreement to take a new lease, the interest arising under the agreement will not be created until such time when the agreement is capable of specific performance. On the facts, the landlord entered into an agreement for a lease with the superior landlord, conditional on the carrying out of repairs by the former, and the repairs had not been carried out. The agreement was held not to be specifically enforceable and accordingly the landlord's interest pursuant to the agreement had not yet been created.

Landlord and Tenant Act 1954, section 41(2)

Where the interest of the landlord is held on trust, the reference to the creation of the interest is a reference to the creation of the trust. There are a few exceptions to this.

Gundry v Stewart (1959)

Where the landlord's interest is held on a trust arising under a will or intestacy, the interest of the landlord will be treated as having been purchased or created when it was purchased or created by or in favour of the deceased testator or intestate.

Morar v Chauhan (1985)

Where the landlord who opposes relies on his own intention to occupy rather than the intention of the beneficiaries under the trust, and he has been landlord for more than five years.

Landlord and Tenant Act 1954, section 42(3)(b)

Where the interest of the landlord is held by a member of a group of companies, the relevant purchase or creation is a purchase from, or creation by, a person other than a member of the group.

VSC Car Park Management Ltd v Regional Railways North East Ltd (2001)

The landlord's interest was transferred back pursuant to a statutory scheme with the landlord taking a lease back so as to remain the tenant's landlord for the purposes of the 1954 Act. It was held that the mischief of the Act was not offended by allowing a landlord who obtains successive tenancies going back over a period of five years to object to the grant of a new tenancy.

8
Disputes as to the terms of a new tenancy

8.1 AGREEMENT AS TO ALL OR SOME OF THE TERMS

In the majority of cases, the parties will settle the terms of the new tenancy by agreement, usually following without prejudice meetings of the respective surveyors. In such cases, the court is bound by the agreed terms in making its order. However, in the absence of agreement, the court will determine the terms which are disputed in accordance with sections 32 to 35 of the *Landlord and Tenant Act* 1954 ('1954 Act'). It often happens that, whilst most of the terms are agreed, the parties remain at odds on one or two issues. In those cases, the court will be bound by the agreed terms and will determine the outstanding matters only.

Derby & Co Ltd v ITC Pension Trust Ltd (1977)

It was held that the court was not bound by terms which had been agreed by the parties 'subject to contract' and 'without prejudice to the tenant's rights under the Act'. Such an agreement was not an agreement for the purposes of sections 32 to 35 of the 1954 Act and the court was free to determine the terms of the new tenancy afresh.

8.2 THE PROPERTY TO BE DEMISED

By section 32(1) of the 1954 Act, the tenant is entitled to a new tenancy of 'the holding' only. The extent of the holding will be determined by reference to the circumstances existing at the date on which an order for the grant of a new tenancy is made.

Landlord and Tenant Act 1954, section 23(3)

Section 23(3) defines 'the holding' as the property comprised in the tenancy excluding any part thereof which is occupied neither by the tenant nor by a person employed by the tenant for the purposes of a business by reason of which the tenancy is one to which Part II of the 1954 Act applies.

In order to establish what the holding is, start by identifying the property demised by the tenancy and look to see which part of that property is occupied by the tenant. Any part which is not so occupied will be excluded from the holding. Occupation is not restricted to business occupation and therefore if a tenant occupies a shop and a flat above, the whole premises will be included in the holding even though the flat is occupied by the tenant for residential purposes. However, if the occupation of an employee is relied upon, the employee's occupation must relate to the business carried out on the premises. In the above scenario, if the manager of the shop lives in the flat, the whole premises will be included but if an employee of the tenant who is employed in respect of a business not connected with the shop occupies the flat, that part of the premises will not form part of the holding.

I & H Caplan Ltd v Caplan (1962)

The House of Lords held that the holding should be determined by an investigation of the facts as at the date of the making of an order for the grant of a new tenancy and not at any earlier time, such as the hearing at first instance or the determination of an appeal on a preliminary point.

Narcissi v Wolfe (1960)

The demised premises included a ground floor, basement and three upper floors. The basement and ground floor were used by the tenant for the purposes of his restaurant business whilst the upper floors were sublet. By the date of the hearing the subtenant of the first floor had vacated and the tenant had begun using the first floor as temporary storage space. It was held that the holding included the first floor in

113

addition to the basement and ground floor and that the motives of the tenant in moving into that space for the purposes of including it in the holding were irrelevant.

Landlord and Tenant Act 1954, section 32(3)

Section 32(3) provides that where the current tenancy includes rights enjoyed by the tenant in connection with the holding, those rights shall be included in the new tenancy unless excluded by agreement or by the court. In the absence of agreement, the court may not enlarge the holding by including rights not already enjoyed by the tenant. However, the court is not bound to include such pre-existing rights and in an appropriate case it may no longer be appropriate to include them.

Re No 1 Albermarle Street, W1 (1959)

A clause permitting the tenant to maintain advertising signs on the exterior of the premises was not a right under section 32(3) but was a 'term' within the meaning of section 35 which could be, and was, included in the new tenancy by the court exercising its discretion.

G Orlik (Meat Products) Ltd v Hastings and Thanet Building Society (1974)

The court had no jurisdiction, whether under sections 32(3) or 35, to include in the new tenancy rights of parking on the landlord's retained land which had not previously been enjoyed by the tenant.

Kirkwood v Johnson (1979)

The court had no jurisdiction under section 32(3) to include a new option to acquire the freehold where the option in the current tenancy had expired without being exercised. To do so would be to enlarge the holding to an impermissible extent.

J Murphy & Sons Ltd v Railtrack plc (2002)

No rights of access could be implied in respect of landlocked premises on renewal under sections 32(3) or 35 of the 1954 Act. Neither section permitted the enlargement of the holding by granting rights not conferred by the previous tenancy.

Landlord and Tenant Act 1954, section 32

Section 32(1A) provides that where the court makes an order for a new tenancy under section 31A(1)(b) of the 1954 Act in a case where the tenant is willing to accept a tenancy of an economically separable part of the holding (in order to avoid successful opposition by the landlord on the grounds of redevelopment), the order for a new tenancy shall only apply to that economically separable part.

Section 32(2) allows the landlord to insist that the whole of the property comprised in the current tenancy is included as opposed to just the holding. This enables a landlord to ensure that his property is not subdivided against his will. However, the landlord must make his election under this section in his acknowledgement of service or claim in accordance with paragraphs 3.7, 3.10 and 3.12 of the Practice Direction to Part 56 of the *Civil Procedure Rules* 1998 ('CPR').

8.3 DURATION OF THE NEW TENANCY

Under section 33 of the 1954 Act, the parties may agree any length of tenancy but in default of agreement, the court shall order a new tenancy for such term as is reasonable in all the circumstances. However, the court may not, in the absence of agreement, make an order for a new fixed term tenancy exceeding 15 years. The maximum period was formerly 14 years but this has been amended by the *Regulatory Reform (Business Tenancies) (England and Wales) Order* 2003 ('2003 Order'). Section 33 of the 1954 Act prescribes that the order for a new tenancy shall be for one beginning on the coming to the end of the current tenancy and the court has no discretion to substitute an alternative commencement date. Where the current tenancy is continued under the Act, the tenancy will only come to an end in accordance with section 64 and the new tenancy will accordingly commence on the day after that on which the current tenancy so determines.

The court has a wide discretion in determining the appropriate length of the tenancy and each case will be determined on its own facts. It must be remembered that the primary purpose of the Act is to protect the tenant's business. However, the factors which it should consider include:

- the length of the current tenancy (including the period of continuation under the Act and the number of previous renewals);
- the fact that the new tenancy will be afforded the protection of the Act;
- the nature of the tenant's business and impact of the length of the term on it;
- the grounds (if any) on which the grant of a new tenancy was opposed especially where the premises are ripe for development or if the landlord desires to occupy the premises for his own business in the near future; and
- the impact on the landlord in having to finding a new tenant in the short term and any likely realisable capital loss the landlord might face if it is intending to sell its reversion.

Re 88 High Road, Kilburn (1959)

The landlord served a section 25 notice specifying that it would oppose the grant of a new tenancy. The tenant made an application for a new tenancy which the landlord then conceded. It was held that since the current tenancy would only come to an end in accordance with section 64, the tenancy could only begin, at the earliest, three months from the date of the hearing.

Upsons Ltd v E Robins Ltd (1956)

The landlord had unsuccessfully opposed the application for a new tenancy on the basis that it intended to occupy the premises itself (ground (g)). The landlord was unsuccessful because it had only been the reversioner for just under the requisite five-year period. The Court of Appeal held that the judge was right to take into account the fact that the landlord wished to occupy and that it might have to leave its existing premises shortly. The tenant wanted a seven-year term but only a one-year term was granted.

Reohorn v Barry Corporation (1956)

The court granted a short fixed term thereafter determinable on six months' notice where the land was ripe for development even though the landlord had failed to prove an immediate intention to redevelop, on the grounds that the 1954 Act should not be used as an instrument to defeat development.

Betty's Cafés Ltd v Phillips Furnishings Stores Ltd (1957)

In deciding upon the term, it is relevant to consider the length of the current tenancy which was the reason given by the Court of Appeal for reducing the term on appeal from 14 years to 5 years. The Court of Appeal decision was upheld on appeal by the House of Lords.

Re Sunlight House, Quay Street, Manchester (1959)

The tenant wanted a term which would have expired only six weeks after the new tenancy commenced. The landlord was contending for a three-year term. It was held that it was relevant to consider the difficulty a landlord might face if he has to re-let the premises after a short time. In that case, the court ordered a term expiring just over six months after the new tenancy commenced, being a reasonable period to enable the landlord to find a new tenant.

London & Provincial Millinery Stores Ltd v Barclays Bank Ltd (1962)

It was held that where premises are ripe for development and the landlord genuinely intends to develop in the near future, any new tenancy should necessarily be of short duration. Therefore in such a case, the Court of Appeal held that the judge had erred in granting a fixed term of nine years and reduced the term to 12 months. The length of the original lease and the length of time that the premises had been occupied by the tenant since the expiry of the term were also relevant considerations to take into account.

Wig Creations Ltd v Colour Film Services Ltd (1969)

The landlord needed the demised premises for its own business but was not able to oppose on ground (g) (own occupation) because it had acquired the reversion less than five years prior to the termination of the original lease under section 30(2). The tenant wanted a long term of 12 years and the evidence was that a shorter term would cause it hardship since it had fitted out the premises and would have to pay more for other premises. The Court of Appeal held that the first instance judge had been right to have regard to the five-year period in section 30(2) in granting a three-year extended lease only.

Michael Chipperfield v Shell UK Ltd (1980)

In exercising its discretion in determining the duration of the term, the court must give proper protection to the tenants but not be unfair to the landlords, nor allow the grant of a new tenancy to defeat development or reduce the value of the building. The court must weigh up and reasonably protect the interests of both parties. An order for a three-year term was upheld on appeal. The Court of Appeal observed that in making the order for a new tenancy the date on which the tenancy was to expire should be expressly stated, given the difficulty in knowing exactly when the tenancy was to commence.

CBS UK Ltd v London Scottish Properties Ltd (1985)

The tenant wanted a short term to enable it to vacate the premises in an orderly way but the landlord contended for a 14-year term. The court gave little weight to the landlord's argument that the grant of a short term would diminish the value of its reversion or to its evidence that in the open market it would be able to achieve a letting of 15 to 20 years with five-yearly reviews. There was no evidence that the landlord was intending to sell its reversion and that it would in fact suffer a realisable loss on sale. Further, the primary purpose of the Act was to protect the tenant who would have had difficulties disposing of a 13-year term. The landlord was properly protected because 11 months gave it sufficient time to find a new tenant and avoid a negative cash flow.

Charles Follett Ltd v Cabtell Investments Ltd (1986)

Following the receipt of advice as to the likely rental on a 14-year term, the tenant requested a one-year term as it wished to keep its options open whilst looking for alternative premises. The first instance judge granted a ten-year term with an option for the tenant to determine the tenancy by six months' notice served not more than one month after the commencement. This part of the decision was not appealed. The rationale behind the order, having regard to the fact that the tenancy would start four months after the date of the order, was to give the tenant five months to find alternative premises and a further six months to vacate.

Peter Millett & Son Ltd v Salisbury Handbags Ltd (1987)

In this case, the previous tenancy had been for a term of 26 weeks with a landlord's break on four weeks' notice. The court ordered a three-year term with a landlord's break clause exercisable by six months' notice expiring at any time but only if a company within the same group as the landlord intended to occupy the shop premises for a business carried on by it. Although the evidence of the landlord's intentions at the hearing was sketchy, the court held that the landlord should be given an opportunity to establish a genuine and workable intention to trade in the shop through its group company.

Ganton House Investments v Crossman Investments (1995)

The previous lease of betting office premises was for a term of 21 years. Shortly before the hearing, the tenant decided it wanted a one-year term rather than 14 years. The landlord wanted 25 years but accepted that the court was limited to a maximum term of 14 years. A term of 14 years with an early tenant's break clause was granted by the court. The following factors were taken into account:

- the length of the original lease;
- the fact that the term originally granted was the usual maximum granted at the time;
- the need for stability;
- the current market conditions; and
- the landlord's evidence that the grant of a short term would very much diminish the capital value of the reversion.

It was held that whilst the tenant should not be able to 'have its cake and eat it', it should be given a reasonable period of time in which to search for new premises and make up its mind whether or not to move.

8.4 TERMS OTHER THAN AS TO PROPERTY, DURATION AND RENT

8.4.1 General principles

Section 35(1) of the 1954 Act provides that, in default of agreement, the court may determine the terms of the tenancy (other than terms as to the duration and the rent payable) and in determining those terms, the court shall have regard to the terms of the current tenancy and to all relevant circumstances. The reference to all relevant circumstances expressly includes a reference to the operation of the provisions of the *Landlord and Tenant (Covenants) Act* 1995 ('1995 Act'). Where the reversion is divided between two or more landlords, terms apportioning the rent may be included.

The starting point is always the terms of the current tenancy but the court should have regard to all relevant circumstances. The onus on establishing that one or more terms of the new tenancy should differ from those of the current tenancy is on the party proposing the relevant term's inclusion, substitution or removal. The change proposed should be a fair and reasonable one.

All of the terms of the tenancy should be settled (whether by agreement or court determination) prior to consideration of the rent payable, since the rent payable will be influenced by the other terms.

O'May v City of London Real Property Co Ltd (1983)

The tenants contended that the terms of the existing tenancy which provided that they should pay a proportion of the heating and lighting expenses of the common parts should be retained whilst the landlords proposed a five-year 'clear lease' whereby the fluctuating costs of the landlords' obligations for maintenance, repair, redecoration and service of the common parts and the structure and exterior of the building would be borne by the tenants. Even though the landlords offered a corresponding reduction in rent, the House of Lords refused to impose more onerous service charge provisions on the tenants. In so doing, their Lordships gave important general guidance as to the proper application of section 35(1) of the 1954 Act:

- the court must begin by considering the terms of the current tenancy which represents the bargain struck by the parties or that imposed by the court on a previous renewal;
- the party proposing departure from those terms must justify its case;
- the court should take into account all the relevant circumstances including the weak negotiating position of a sitting tenant and the purpose of the Act which is to protect the tenant's business interests at the end of the term;
- changes will not be accepted if they are not reasonable and the issue is whether the change can be justified on grounds of essential fairness between the parties;
- to impose long-term risks on the tenants was not proportionate to the relative interests of the parties in the property even though the landlords were offering a corresponding reduction in rent.

Boots the Chemists Ltd v Pinkland (1992)

Applying the principles set out in the *O'May* case (above), the judge refused to depart from the terms of the current tenancy by deleting the inclusion of a positive trading covenant. The onus was on the tenant to justify such a departure and the positive trading covenant benefited both the landlord and other tenants.

Amarjee v Barrowfen Properties Ltd (1993)

In this case, the current tenancy had been made orally and did not contain the comprehensive covenants one would expect in a written tenancy agreement. In departing from the terms of the oral tenancy the judge expressed the view that de facto terms which may be deduced from the conduct of the parties during the operation of an informal tenancy were of far less weight than the express terms of a formal lease.

8.4.2 Break clauses

The issue of whether a break clause should be included is closely related to the question as to the appropriate length of term to be granted. Where one party desires a long term it may be of considerable advantage to it to offer the inclusion of a break provision, most often restricted in terms of the circumstances in which it can be exercised. The law in this area has particularly focussed on redevelopment break clauses and in general it must be remembered that the 1954 Act seeks to provide a balance by conferring reasonable security of tenure on business tenants whilst at the same time not unduly restricting legitimate development. In general, a redevelopment break clause will often be justified in cases where the premises are 'ripe for development' even where the landlord's opposition on ground (f) has been unsuccessful or such opposition has not been advanced.

Reohorn v Barry Corporation (1956)

The court granted a short fixed term thereafter determinable on six months' notice where the land was ripe for development even though the landlord had failed to prove an immediate intention to redevelop, on grounds that the 1954 Act should not be used as an instrument to defeat development.

Adams v Green (1978)

The court ordered a new lease for a term of 14 years with a landlord's break clause exercisable at any time on two years' notice. Whilst the premises were not 'ripe for development' in the sense that the landlords had no intention to develop the premises themselves and had produced no evidence of the viability of development, the possibility of the landlord or their successors in title wishing to carry out such future development was sufficiently likely to justify the inclusion of a break notice. Stamp LJ said that it was not the policy of the 1954 Act to give security to the tenant at the expense of preventing redevelopment.

Annika Motors v Colebrook Holdings Ltd (1981)

Even though the landlord had an immediate intention to redevelop, the court ordered a three-year term with no break clause because following receipt of a section 25 notice, which indicated that the landlord did not intend to oppose the grant of a new tenancy, the tenant had invested heavily in the premises.

JH Edwards v Central London Commercial Estates (1984)

The first instance judge was satisfied that there was a possibility of a bona fide decision to operate a break clause in future but did not insert a break clause into tenancies of ten and twelve years' duration. The Court of Appeal indicated that if the landlords might wish to develop they should not be saddled with a lease which prevented such development and it was wrong in such cases to grant tenancies for substantial terms with no redevelopment break clauses. In that case, redevelopment break clauses exercisable at the fifth year of the term were inserted.

Becker v Hill Street Properties Ltd (1990)

Where the landlord would have been ready to redevelop about one year after the grant of the new tenancy, the Court of Appeal upheld the grant of a new tenancy for a four-and-a-half year term which coincided with the date upon which the tenant wished to retire.

National Car Parks v Paternoster Square (1990)

Whilst there were considerable difficulties in the way of the future development proposed by the landlord, in that planning permission had not been obtained and there were issues surrounding the right to vacant possession of part of the development site, the Vice-Chancellor was satisfied that there was a real possibility (as distinct from a probability) that the landlord would redevelop the site. The court ordered the inclusion of a general redevelopment break clause exercisable at any time on six months' notice. The tenant was adequately protected by the Act in that on exercising the break the landlord would still have to establish ground (f) and that could involve a considerable time lag.

Davy's of London (Wine Merchants) Ltd v City of London Corporation (2004)

The test for considering whether a redevelopment break clause should be inserted in a new tenancy involved two propositions, namely that, so far as reasonable:

(i) a new tenancy should not prevent a landlord from developing; and
(ii) reasonable degree of security should be provided to the tenant.

Lewison J took into account new evidence submitted on the appeal (which was by way of a rehearing), the appeal date being the relevant date for determining the terms of the new tenancy. A break clause was inserted in terms which allowed for the landlord's 'fall back exit strategy' of a sale to a developer within two to four years.

8.4.3 Repairing obligations and service charges

Whilst each case will turn on its own facts, it will rarely be appropriate to offset the cost of repair or shift the burden of repair onto the tenant in cases where the landlord is liable for those costs under the current tenancy. However, there may be cases in which the court will consider it reasonable to update existing service charge provisions to modernise them or to remove obsolete provisions. Conversely, it will rarely be appropriate to delete service charge provisions so as to make the landlord liable for costs he would previously have been able to recover from the tenant. Terms as to service charges should be considered under section 35(1) of the 1954 Act even if those charges are reserved as rent.

Bullen v Goodland (1961)

This case contains judicial statements to the effect that where a short term is granted, responsibility for the structure should normally be left out of the terms of the new lease. However, it is unclear what repairing covenants (if any) were contained in the old tenancy. It is thought that this case should not be used as authority for removing a tenant's repairing obligation if under the current tenancy he is so liable even if a short term is granted on renewal.

Hyams v Titan Properties (1972)

The Court of Appeal, in an inflationary market, substituted a variable service charge provision in place of the obligation in the current tenancy to make a fixed contribution.

[This is questionable in light of the *O'May* decision (see 8.4.1 above).]

O'May v City of London Real Property Co Ltd (1983)

The House of Lords refused to impose the costs of repair and decoration of the structure, exterior and common parts of the building onto the tenants against their will even where the landlord was prepared to accept a lower rent. In particular, it was held disproportionate to impose on the tenants, who were taking a relatively short-term lease, long-term risks which would usually be borne by the landlords.

Leslie and Godwin Investments Ltd v Prudential Assurance Company Ltd (1987)

The landlord was willing to consent to a deletion in the current service charge provisions so as to exclude any contribution from the tenant for maintenance, repair and redecoration of the building and for long-term repairs of the lifts and boiler installations. The tenant contended that no service charge should be payable at all. The court held that, whatever the length of the tenancy, there was no prospect that the court would consider that it was reasonable to remove the tenant's liability to pay the service charge completely.

Amarjee v Barrowfen Properties Ltd (1993)

On renewal of an oral periodic tenancy by a new fixed-term 14-year tenancy it was held that the tenant should pay a service charge in respect of the parade of shops of which it formed part, there being, in the judge's opinion, no practicable alternative. In departing from the terms of the oral tenancy, the judge held that de facto terms which may be deduced from the conduct of the parties, during the creation of an informal tenancy, are of far less weight than the express terms of a formal lease.

8.4.4 User covenants

Generally speaking, the court will not sanction changes to the user covenants merely to enable one of the parties to gain a rental advantage but each case must be decided on its own merits and in some cases it may be appropriate to alter the terms as to user. It must be borne in mind that the extent of the user covenant is an important factor in the assignability of the tenancy, but the court will not readily widen the user clause merely to confer on the tenant a more saleable asset.

Davis v Brighton Corporation (1956)

The fact that the tenant has been conducting his business in breach of user covenant does not justify the inclusion of a wider covenant in the new tenancy so as to make such user lawful. The tenant must apply to the landlord for a change of use.

Gold v Brighton Corporation (1956)

Where the current tenancy included an open user covenant, the Court of Appeal restricted the user to the tenant's business as a dealer in new and secondhand furs and ladies' and children's wear. Two points of principle emerge:

- the primary purpose of the 1954 Act is to protect the tenant in his business and strong and cogent evidence is required to restrict him carrying on an important part of it and on that basis the landlord failed in its attempt to prohibit secondhand sales;
- however, the purpose of the Act is not to confer on the tenant a 'new saleable asset' and it was therefore not appropriate to insert in the new tenancy the former widely drafted user clause.

Aldwych Club Ltd v Copthall Property Co Ltd (1962)

The user clause in the current lease restricted use to that of a club unless the landlord consented to any other use, such consent not to be unreasonably refused. There was scope for the premises to be used as offices. The tenant only wished to use the premises as a club and sought to remove the proviso so as to reduce the rental payable on renewal. The court refused to remove the proviso merely to enable the tenant to obtain a rental advantage.

Charles Clements (London) Ltd v Rank City Wall Ltd (1978)

The current tenancy restricted use to the tenant's business as a cutler. The landlord wanted to include a proviso that the landlord's consent to a change of use was not to be unreasonably withheld in order to increase the rent payable. The court refused to include the proviso so as to relax the user covenant against the tenant's wishes. It was not reasonable to increase the rent by widening the user clause beyond that which the tenant required in order to carry out its business, even though its inclusion would have increased the assignability of the tenancy.

Boots the Chemist Ltd v Pinkland (1992)

The court refused to delete a positive 'keep open' covenant since the covenant was of value to the landlord and other tenants in the shopping centre.

Amarjee v Barrowfen Properties Ltd (1993)

The existing tenancy was oral and contained no terms so the user permitted was open. The court restricted user to that of the tenant's business selling furniture and carpets even though the tenant's motivation was to obtain a rental advantage. The position would probably have been different had the current tenancy been in writing.

8.4.5 Alienation provisions

A landlord seeking to restrict an alienation clause on renewal must show very powerful reasons for so doing. Likewise the purpose of the 1954 Act is to protect the business of the tenant and not to confer on him a saleable asset and the court will be rarely widen the user covenant merely to increase assignability. Consideration must be given to the effect of the 1995 Act since all tenancies granted on renewal will be 'new tenancies' within that Act and in general terms a tenant will not remain liable on the covenants following assignment. In most cases, it will be reasonable for a landlord to insist that an authorised guarantee agreement ('AGA') is entered into on assignment, but only in so far as it is reasonable to require an AGA under the 1995 Act.

Cardshops Ltd v Davies (1971)

The Court of Appeal allowed a tenant's appeal against the inclusion in the new tenancy of a qualified covenant against assignment subject to a proviso to the effect that in the event of the tenant contemplating an assignment it would first offer to surrender the term for no consideration. There were no special reasons justifying so novel and burdensome a departure from the terms of the original lease which contained a standard qualified covenant against assignment without any such proviso.

Turone v Howard de Walden Estates Ltd (No 1) (1982)

It was right to exclude from the terms of the new lease a clause which would prohibit assignment or subletting of part of the demised premises where the opinion of both experts was that, given the layout of the premises, such a partial assignment or subletting was not practicable in any event.

Amarjee v Barrowfen Properties Ltd (1993)

The tenant sought to include in the new lease a clause which would relieve it of continuing liability following assignment. The judge refused to include such a non-recourse alienation provision which he found would be almost unheard of and which would have a potentially adverse effect on the value of the reversion. It should be noted that this case was decided prior to the 1995 Act.

Landlord and Tenant Act 1954, section 35(2)

Section 35(2) expressly provides that the reference to all relevant circumstances in section 35(1) includes a reference to the operation of the provisions of the 1995 Act.

Landlord and Tenant (Covenants) Act 1995

Previously, tenants were often concerned that under the doctrine of privity of contract they would remain liable on the covenants in the renewed tenancy even after an assignment. This frequently explained a tenant's motivation in seeking a short term as the courts were reluctant to include terms restricting liability to the time in which the renewed lease remained vested in it. However, the 1995 Act restricts the tenant's liability in respect of 'new leases' to the time that the lease is vested in it. All tenancies ordered by the court under the 1954 Act are 'new tenancies' for the purpose of the 1995 Act. By section 16 of the 1995 Act, the landlord may require the tenant to enter into an authorised guarantee agreement (an AGA) on assignment. However, the landlord may only demand an AGA if (1) the lease requires an AGA as a condition to assignment, or (2) it is reasonable for him to require the tenant to execute such a deed. Further, an AGA can only extend to the time in which the lease is vested in the immediate assignee and therefore expires on a successive assignment of the term.

Wallis Fashion Group Ltd v CGU Life Assurance Ltd (2000)

The landlord sought to include a requirement that the tenant provide an AGA as a condition to consent to assignment, whereas the tenant contended the landlord should only be able to require an AGA where it was reasonable to do so. The court held in favour of the tenant. Where the lease was silent as to the landlord's right to demand an AGA, the landlord was not automatically entitled to require one when his consent was sought. The standard of reasonableness was not burdensome to the landlord since the tenant would have to show that no reasonable landlord could, in the circumstances, require it. Neuberger J indicated that it was unattractive for a landlord to contend that he should be entitled to the benefit of a covenant which entitled him to be unreasonable. In that case, evidence tended to demonstrate that market forces demanded the type of covenant sought by the landlord and all but one of the other tenants had agreed to the form of covenant proposed by the landlord. Whilst, in estate management terms, it was mildly more convenient for a landlord to have all leases in a given development in similar terms, in this case there was no specific evidence that the landlord would encounter any real estate management difficulties if one tenancy was in slightly different terms, and the court accordingly gave little weight to this factor.

8.4.6 Guarantors

Express provision is made for the situation where only one of two or more joint tenants formerly in partnership obtains a new tenancy. It appears that in other cases, the court may require the provision of a guarantee under section 35 of the 1954 Act. The court is more likely to impose such a requirement where the landlord had the benefit of a guarantee in respect of the tenant's liabilities under the current tenancy and where it can be shown that the tenant has been recently incorporated or is of doubtful financial standing. As is the case with all terms, each case will turn on its own facts.

Landlord and Tenant Act 1954, section 41A(6)

Where the court makes an order under section 29 of the 1954 Act for the grant of a new tenancy, it may order the grant to be made to such of the tenants as are actually running the business, or to them jointly with the persons carrying on the business in partnership with them, and may order the grant to be made subject to the satisfaction, within a time specified by the order, of such conditions as to guarantors, sureties or otherwise as appear to the court to be equitable, having regard to the omission of the other joint tenants from the persons who will be the tenants under the new tenancy.

Cairnplace Ltd v CBL (Property Investment) Company Ltd (1984)

It was held that the court had jurisdiction under section 35 of the 1954 Act to include a term in the new lease requiring the tenant to provide guarantors in respect of his obligations. In that case, the alienation provisions in the current tenancy required the giving of two directors' guarantees on assignment and the evidence demonstrated that the tenant company had only recently been incorporated and had a low profit margin and considerable debts.

8.4.7 Costs of leases

The court has no jurisdiction to include in the new lease a term requiring the tenant to pay the costs of the new lease even if the current tenancy so provides.

Cairnplace Ltd v CBL (Property Investment) Company Ltd (1984)

It was held that the court should not require the tenant to pay the costs of the new lease, even where the current tenancy contains a term to that effect because the court will not deprive the tenant of his rights under the *Cost of Leases Act* 1958 which provides that the tenant can only be liable for such costs where the parties have expressly so provided.

8.5 DETERMINATION OF RENT

8.5.1 General

In the absence of the parties' agreement as to the rent to be payable under the new tenancy, the court has power to determine the rent under section 34 of the 1954 Act. The court will determine the rent according to the valuation formula with the assistance of expert evidence and does not have a general discretion to determine the rent. It is not appropriate for the court to consider the question of rent whilst the other terms of the new tenancy remain disputed. Since the other terms will dictate the appropriate rental that could be achieved on an open market letting, the rent payable should be considered last. However, in a case where one or more of the other terms are disputed, it is usual for the parties to agree or produce expert evidence of the appropriate rentals on alternative bases which take into account the different hypotheses as to the other terms to be included. Sometimes the various hypothetical rentals can be agreed, leaving the court with only the task of determining the other terms of the lease.

Cardshops Ltd v Davies (1971)

The Court of Appeal confirmed that it is inappropriate for the court to determine the rent until the parties have agreed or the court has determined the extent of the holding, the length of the term and the other terms of the tenancy as each of those factors will affect the rent payable under section 34.

Fawke v Viscount Chelsea (1980)

It was held that the court has jurisdiction under section 34 to assess a differential rent which increases by fixed amounts.

O'May v City of London Real Property Ltd (1983)

The House of Lords highlighted the differences between sections 34 and 35(1) of the 1954 Act. Whilst under section 35(1), the court retains a wide discretion as to the other terms of the tenancy under section 34, the court is confined to determining the rent according to the statutory formula with the assistance of expert evidence.

Giannolcalous v Saltfleet Ltd (1988)

The court confirmed that in determining the rent under section 34, the court exercises no discretion and is not able to reduce the rent determined in accordance with the valuation formula in section 34 to a level that the tenant can afford.

8.5.2 Date of valuation

The valuation date is the date of commencement of the new tenancy. This will usually be three months and two weeks after the date of the hearing at which the court determines the rent and makes the order for a new tenancy, by virtue of the provisions relating to termination of continuation tenancies set out in section 64 of the 1954 Act. The court should therefore assess the rent based on the best evidence at the date of the hearing, including evidence as to any probable changes in the market between the date of the hearing and the likely date of commencement of the new tenancy.

English Exporters v Eldonwall (1973)

Megarry J indicated that a determination of rent under section 34 was necessarily prospective as the court was fixing a new rent as from the future commencement of a new tenancy.

Lovely & Orchard Services Ltd v Daejan Investments (Grove Hall) Ltd (1978)

The duty of the court in determining the rent under section 34 is to determine the rent under that section as at the date of hearing but having regard to such evidence as there may be that indicates that changes are likely to occur between the date of the hearing and the date of commencement of the new tenancy (assuming that the order will be effective). The court has to ask itself at what rent the premises might reasonably be expected to be let in the open market by a willing lessor for a term commencing on that commencement date.

8.5.3 **The valuation formula**

A valuer instructed to advise or provide a report as to the appropriate rental on a lease renewal should refer to the precise valuation formula set out in section 34 of the 1954 Act.

Under section 34, the rent payable is that which, having regard to the terms of the new tenancy (other than those relating to rent), the holding might reasonably be expected to be let in the open market by a willing lessor.

Section 34 sets out four statutory disregards which are dealt with in more detail below.

8.5.4 **Open market letting: assumptions**

In determining the open market letting:

- regard must be had to the terms of the new tenancy (other than those relating to rent);
- it should be assumed that there is both a willing vendor and a willing purchaser;
- it should be assumed that the premises are let with vacant possession although if the premises to be comprised in the new tenancy are sublet, the valuation must take account of those subtenancies;
- by section 34(4) of the 1954 Act any effect on rent of the operation of the 1995 Act must be taken into account. In most cases, this will predominantly be the effect of the 1995 Act in releasing the tenant from liability on an assignment, or on a subsequent assignment if an AGA is executed.

Harewood Hotels v Harris (1958)

The effect of disregarding the tenant's occupation is that the premises have to be envisaged as empty premises in the market.

Aldwych Club Ltd v Copthall Property Co Ltd (1962)

The user clause limited use of the premises to that of a gentleman's club, subject to change of use with the landlord's consent (such consent not to be unreasonably withheld). The court was satisfied that the landlord could not refuse consent to change of use to offices and determined the rent on the basis that the premises could be used as offices.

Oscroft v Benabo (1967)

In determining the rent, the court took into account the fact that upper parts of the premises were subject to a residential subtenancy at a controlled rent.

Evans v English Electric (1973)

In the context of rent review, the 'willing lessor' and 'willing lessee' were described as abstractions, namely hypothetical persons who were willing (but not anxious) to reach agreement. The personal circumstances of the actual landlord and tenant are irrelevant.

Plinth Property Investments Ltd v Mott, Hay & Anderson (1979)

The court will assume for the purposes of valuation that the hypothetical lessor will enforce any absolute user covenant such that the possibility that the lessor might relax the covenant should be ignored.

Family Management v Gray (1980)

Whilst premises are to be valued in their actual condition, a tenant cannot rely on its own failure to comply with its repairing obligation to contend for a lower rent.

Northern Electric v Addison plc (1997)

Where the user clause restricted the use of premises as an electricity substation the valuation exercise required one to assume that the notional lessor was willing to let the premises as such without demanding a premium to take into account other potential uses.

8.5.5 **Open market letting: disregards**

8.5.5.1 **General**

Section 34(1) expressly requires the court to disregard four matters namely:

(1) Any effect on rent of the fact that the tenant has or his predecessors have been in occupation of the holding.
(2) Any goodwill attached to the holding by reason of the carrying on thereat of the business of the tenant (whether by him or by a predecessor of his in that business).
(3) Any effect on rent of a 'tenant's improvement' to which the section applies (as to which, see 8.5.5.2 below).
(4) In respect of licensed premises, any value attributable to a licence belonging to the tenant. For these purposes, where Part II of the 1954 Act applies by virtue of section 23(1A), reference to the tenant includes a company in which the tenant has a controlling interest or where the tenant is a company includes a person with a controlling interest in the company.

Cramas Properties Ltd v Connaught Furs Trimmings Ltd (1965)

It is only the goodwill attributable to the particular business carried on by the tenant which is to be disregarded, not the kind of business carried on at the premises.

J Murphy & Sons Ltd v Railtrack plc (2002)

On renewal of a tenancy of landlocked premises, the Court of Appeal held that it was not appropriate to disregard the lack of access in determining the rent under section 34. It was held that disregarding the lack of access would have the result that the tenant would be forced to pay the landlord for an access right that the tenant already possessed by reason of its ownership of adjoining land and that the landlord had no power to grant. Section 34 expressly set out the statutory disregards and it was not possible to include other disregards by implication.

8.5.5.2 Disregard of tenant's improvements

Under section 34(2), the statutory disregard of tenant's improvements only applies to improvements which:

- were carried out by a person who was the tenant when they were carried out; and
- were carried out by the tenant otherwise than in pursuance of obligation to his immediate landlord; and
- were either carried out during the current tenancy or, if they were not carried out during the current tenancy, satisfy the further conditions set out below.

The further conditions are that the improvement was completed not more than 21 years before the application to the court was made and that the holding or any part of it affected by the improvement has at all times since the completion of the improvement been comprised in tenancies of the description specified in section 23(1) of the Act and that at the termination of each of those tenancies the tenant did not quit.

New Zealand Government Property Corporation Ltd v HM & S Ltd (1982)

Removable tenant's fixtures are not 'improvements' but also are not treated as forming part of the demised premises which are valued.

Durley House Ltd v Cadogan (2000)

It was held that the improvements are 'carried out by the tenant' within the meaning of section 34(2) where they are carried out by a third party under a contract or other arrangement with the tenant even though the tenant does not pay for the improvements.

8.5.6 Rent review provisions

Section 34(3) of the 1954 Act expressly provides that where the rent is determined by the court, the court may, if it thinks fit, determine that the terms of the tenancy shall include such provisions for varying the rent as may be specified in the determination.

The question of the appropriate periods for rent review is a matter for the discretion of the court. The court is influenced by market practice and will usually hear evidence as to what pattern of rent review is acceptable in respect of premises of the type and location of the demised premises. However, the object of the exercise is to strike a fair balance between landlord and tenant and the courts are disinclined to order upwards-only reviews.

Stylo Shoes Ltd v Manchester Royal Exchange (1967)

In respect of a 14-year term, the court rejected the landlord's claim for an upwards-only rent review and inserted an upwards-and-downwards rent review.

Jane's (Gowns) Ltd v Harlow Development Corporation (1980)

Evidence of the market in the locality of the demised premises indicated that rent could go up or down in future. The court inserted an upwards-and-downwards rent review clause but did not make any adjustment in the rent to reflect the insertion of the review provisions.

Blythewood Plant Hire Ltd v Spiers Ltd (1992)

The court found on the evidence that insertion of an upwards-and-downwards rent review would have an immediate impact on the value of the landlords' reversion and ordered an upwards-only review at the end of the fifth year of a ten-year term. The evidence in that case was that a tenant would not pay substantially more rent for the insertion of an upwards-and-downwards clause.

Boots the Chemists Ltd v Pinkland (1992)

The court inserted an upwards-and-downwards rent review clause at the end of the fifth and tenth years of a 14-year term. It was noted that rents which can only be reviewed upwards can wreak injustice on tenants in a falling market whereas an upwards-and-downwards review would not prejudice the landlord.

Amarjee v Barrowfen Properties Ltd (1993)

The court inserted an upwards-and-downwards rent review clause indicating that such clauses have the obvious merit of fairness.

Fourboys plc v Newport Borough Council (1994)

The court inserted a three-yearly upwards-and-downwards review provision in respect of a nine-year term of a shop unit even though other units in the shopping centre had been let on the open market with upwards-only reviews. The judge considered that the insertion of an upwards-and-downwards review was fair to both the landlord and the tenant.

9
Preparing and giving expert evidence

9.1 CONTENTS OF THE REPORT

Under the *Civil Procedure Rules* 1998 ('CPR'), Rule 35.5 expert evidence must be given in a written report unless the court directs otherwise.

The content of the expert report will depend on the circumstances of the case. An expert may wish to prepare a draft report and discuss its contents with a solicitor or counsel before it is exchanged in final form.

The report must comply with the requirements of PD 35 and must be verified by the following statement of truth:

> 'I believe that the facts I have stated in this report are true and that the opinions I have expressed are correct.'

The report must be addressed to the court and not to the party by whom the expert has been instructed and contain the following information:

- details of his qualifications;
- details of literature or other material which the expert has relied on in making the report;
- identification and relevant qualifications of the person who has carried out any test or experiment which the expert has used for the report and whether or not the test or experiment has been carried out under the expert's supervision;
- a summary of the range of opinion and reasons for his own opinion where there is a range of opinion on matters dealt with in the report;
- a summary of the conclusions reached;
- a statement that the expert understands his duty to the court and has complied with that duty;

- a statement setting out the substance of all material instructions (written or oral) summarising the facts and instructions given to the expert, which are material to the opinions expressed in the report or upon which those opinions are based.

Although those instructions given to an expert are not protected by privilege (CPR 35.10(4)), an expert cannot be cross-examined on the contents of his instructions without the consent of the party who gave the instructions, or the permission of the court. If the court is satisfied that there are reasonable grounds to believe that the statement in the report setting out the substance of the instructions is inaccurate or incomplete, it will allow cross-examination where it appears to be in the interests of justice to do so (CPR 35.10(4), PD 35, paragraph 3).

9.2   DUTIES AS AN EXPERT – OVERRIDING DUTY TO THE COURT

9.2.1 Procedural rules

Civil Procedure Rules 1998, Rule 35.3

- It is the duty of an expert to help the court on the matters within his expertise.
- This duty overrides any obligation to the person from whom he has received instructions or by whom he is paid.

Civil Procedure Rules 1998, Part 35

- An expert witness is under an overriding duty to help the court with its overriding obligation under CPR Rule 1.1(1) to deal with the case 'justly':

    '1.1(2) Dealing with a case justly includes, so far as is practicable–

    (a) ensuring that the parties are on an equal footing;
    (b) saving expense;
    (c) dealing with the case in ways which are proportionate–

        (i)   to the amount of money involved;
        (ii) to the importance of the case;
        (iii) to the complexity of the issues; and
        (iv) to the financial position of each party;

(d) ensuring that it is dealt with expeditiously and fairly; and

(e) allotting to it an appropriate share of the court's resources ... '.

Crown copyright material is reproduced with the permission of the Controller of HMSO and the Queen's Printer for Scotland.

9.2.2 General principles

- Some courts have published their own guides which supplement the CPR for proceedings in those courts. These contain provisions affecting expert evidence and an expert witness should be familiar with them when they are relevant to his evidence.
- Any advice given by an expert before court proceedings are started is likely to be confidential to the client and privileged from disclosure to other parties. But where the expert is asked to give or prepare evidence for the purpose of court proceedings, so that Part 35 applies, he is required to state the substance of the instructions he has received. The court has the power to order the expert to disclose what his or her instructions were.
- Although the point has yet to be definitively decided, the power to order disclosure may in certain circumstances extend to instructions or advice that were privileged when they were given.
- The expert should also be aware that any failure by him to comply with the Rules or court orders or any excessive delay for which the expert is responsible may result in the party who instructed him being penalised in costs and even in extreme cases being debarred from placing the expert's evidence before the court.

Experts should have regard to the RICS *Practice Statement and Guidance Note: Surveyors Acting as Expert Witnesses* and the *Code of Guidance on Expert Evidence: A Guide for Experts and Those Instructing Them for the Purpose of Court Proceedings*. The latter code was published in December 2001 to facilitate better communication and dealings both between the expert and the instructing party and between the parties; as such it is drawn in general terms so as to provide guidance for every court of law in the Civil Jurisdiction and in every type of civil litigation.

Stevens v Gullis (1999)

If an expert witness completely disregards his duty to the court by failing to follow the court's directions, the court may rule that the party may not rely on that expert's evidence, the effect of which may mean that the party loses the entire action.

Pride Valley Foods Ltd v Hall and Partners (2001)

The judge was very critical of an expert witness in a construction case whose report was more than 200 pages in length, and which included opinions on issues outside his expertise:

> ' ... his report offends the established basis on which an expert should give evidence'.

National Justice Compania Naviera Surrey Aviation v Prudential Assurance Company Ltd ('The Ikarian Reefer') (1993)

Cresswell J considered the case law as to the duties and responsibilities of experts, in relation to the court and to the party:

- Evidence given by the expert must be independent and not influenced by the litigation – *Whitehouse v Jordan* (1981).
- The expert witness must provide independent assistance to the court by way of objective unbiased opinion in relation to matters within his expertise – *Polivette Ltd v Commercial Union Assurance Company plc* (1987).
- The expert witness should state the facts or assumptions on which his opinion is based. He should not omit to include material facts which could detract from his concluded opinion. He should never assume the role of an advocate – *Re Jay* (1990).
- An expert witness should make it clear when a particular question or issue falls outside his area of expertise.

- If an expert's opinion is not properly researched because he considers that insufficient data are available then this must be stated with an indication that the opinion is no more than a provisional one – *Re Jay* (1990).
- Where the expert who has prepared a report cannot assert that the report contains the truth the whole truth and nothing but the truth without some qualification, that qualification should be stated in the report – *Darby & Co Ltd v Welldon (No. 9)* (1990).
- If, after exchange of reports, an expert witness changes his view on the material having read the other side's expert report or for any other reason, such change of view should be communicated (through legal representatives), to the other side without delay and when appropriate to the court.
- Where expert evidence refers to photographs, plans, calculations, analyses, measurements survey reports or other similar documents, these must be provided to the opposite party at the same time as the exchange of reports.

Anglo Group plc v Winther Brown and Co Ltd (2000)

Expert witnesses should make it clear whether any question or issue falls outside their expertise, or their conclusions are based on inadequate evidence. When an expert receives new information he should be prepared to reconsider and even change his mind.

The following propositions also arose from that case:

- The independent assistance must be provided to the court at all stages of the proceedings. This applies as much to the initial meeting of experts as to evidence at the trial.
- The expert's evidence should normally be confined to technical matters on which the court will be assisted by receiving an explanation, or to evidence or common professional practice.
- The expert witness should not give evidence or opinions as to what he himself would have done in the circumstances or otherwise seek to usurp the role of the judge.
- The expert should co-operate with the other parties in an attempt to narrow the technical issues in dispute at the earliest opportunity and to eliminate or place in context any peripheral issues.

- The expert should co-operate with the other expert(s) in attending without prejudice meetings as necessary and in seeking to find areas of agreement and to define precisely areas of disagreement to be set out in a joint statement of experts ordered by the court.
- The evidence presented to the court should be, and be seen to be, the independent product of the expert uninfluenced as to form or content by the exigencies of litigation.
- An expert should be ready to reconsider his opinion and if appropriate to change his mind when he has received new information or has considered the opinion of the other expert. He should do so at the earliest opportunity.

Pearce v Ove Arup Partnership (2001)

If an expert does not comply with his duty to the court to be objective and acts like an advocate, the trial judge is likely to criticise the expert and discount the evidence, but may also refer the expert's conduct to his professional body – see *Stevens v Gullis* below.

Stevens v Gullis (1999)

An expert who had demonstrated a total lack of understanding of the duties and requirements of the court as regards experts was debarred from acting as a witness in the proceedings.

9.3 MEETING THE OTHER SURVEYOR

The expert may find it helpful to meet the other side's surveyor to discuss the issues in dispute.

Civil Procedure Rules 1998, Rule 35.12

The court may direct discussions between experts for the purpose of requiring them to:

- identify and discuss the expert issues in the proceedings; and
- where possible, reach an agreed opinion on those issues.

The court may specify the issues which the experts must discuss and may direct that following a discussion, the experts prepare a statement for the court showing those issues on which they agree and those issues on which they disagree with a summary of their reasons for disagreeing. The content of the discussion between the experts shall not be referred to at the trial unless the parties agree. Where experts reach agreement on an issue during their discussions, the agreement shall not bind the parties unless the parties expressly agree to be bound by the agreement.

This rule can be seen as an aspect of encouraging the parties to co-operate in the conduct of the proceedings, which is part of the active case management criteria in CPR Rule 1.4(2)(a).

Discussions between experts may be held voluntarily and without any direction from the court.

Robin Ellis Ltd v Malwright Ltd (1999)

Where the court directs a discussion between experts and gives specific directions concerning that discussion, compliance with those specific directions is a condition to be satisfied before the evidence of the experts may be admitted at trial. Interference by the parties in telling the experts what opinions they are allowed to hold in complying with a direction to prepare a joint statement may amount to a breach of the condition with the result that permission to adduce the expert's evidence at trial may be refused.

10
Compensation on quitting the holding

10.1 COMPENSATION GENERALLY

The policy of the *Landlord and Tenant Act* 1954 ('1954 Act') is to allow landlords to oppose the grant of a new tenancy on certain grounds which are not fault-based, namely on grounds (e) (subletting of part), (f) (redevelopment) and (g) (landlord's occupation) (as are dealt with in more detail in Chapter 7). However, where the tenant is effectively precluded from having the benefit of a new tenancy by reason of one or more of these non-fault-based grounds it will be entitled to compensation for disturbance on quitting the holding. Compensation is not payable where the landlord successfully opposes the grant of a new tenancy on fault-based grounds such as grounds (a) (disrepair), (b) (persistent delay in paying rent), or (c) (other substantial breaches of covenant).

Whilst this chapter is primarily concerned with compensation for disturbance as described above, in some cases a business tenant will also be entitled on quitting the premises to claim compensation for certain improvements under Part I of the *Landlord and Tenant Act* 1927 ('1927 Act'). A detailed examination of the 1927 Act is beyond the scope of this work. If Part I applies, the tenant or his predecessor must have given notice of their intention to make an improvement before the relevant improvements were carried out in order to claim compensation. There are strict time limits in which a claim to such compensation must be made. In the renewal context, the time limits are set out in section 47 of the 1954 Act. Such a claim must be made within three months of the service of a section 25 notice (or landlord's counter-notice in response to a section 26 request or if no counter-notice is given within three months of the last date on which such a notice could have been given). Consideration should therefore be given to the question of a possible claim for compensation at the outset of the renewal process.

10.2 **WHEN COMPENSATION FOR DISTURBANCE IS PAYABLE**

Section 37(1) to 37(1C) of the 1954 Act provides that on quitting the holding, the tenant is entitled to compensation in three 'compensation cases', namely:

(1) where the tenant's renewal application is declined by the court because the landlord has made out one or more of the grounds in (e), (f) or (g) of section 30(1) (the compensation grounds) but not other grounds; or

(2) where the landlord has commenced termination proceedings under section 29(2) and the court is precluded from making an order a new tenancy by reason of any of the compensation grounds and not by reason of any other grounds; and

(3) where the landlord has indicated its opposition (on any of the compensation grounds and not on any other grounds) to the tenant having a new tenancy in its section 25 notice or counter-notice to the tenant's section 26 request and either no application has been made under sections 24(1) or 29(2) or, if such an application has been made, it has been withdrawn.

10.3 **TACTICS**

There is a clear advantage to a landlord in relying on fault-based grounds of opposition in addition to the compensation grounds. If such additional grounds are specified and the tenant does not make an application or fails to pursue the matter to a final substantive hearing, no compensation will be payable. The landlord might consider that the tenant will give up and quit the premises without contesting the fault-based grounds of opposition. However, there must be some basis for relying on other grounds since if the landlord does include additional grounds without any cause such inclusion may well invalidate the notice for lack of good faith. Further, the court is empowered to subsequently award damages to the tenant if it is induced to quit the holding by reason of any misrepresentation or concealment of material facts by the landlord.

On the other hand, a tenant who does not wish to renew may serve a section 26 request and pursue an application for a new tenancy purely to obtain compensation.

De Havilland v Centrovincial (1971)

If a landlord only specifies his opposition on one of the compensation grounds in his section 25 notice or counter-notice, he will be liable to pay compensation to the tenant if it does not make an application for a new tenancy and may not avoid liability to pay compensation by notifying the tenant of his withdrawal of opposition.

Sun Life Assurance plc v Thales Tracs Ltd (2001)

The Court of Appeal held that a tenant may make a section 26 request purely to obtain compensation since there was no requirement in section 26 that the tenant need state his intention or belief.

10.4 COMPENSATION ONLY PAYABLE WHEN THE TENANT QUITS THE HOLDING

Compensation is not payable to the tenant until the tenant has physically yielded up possession of the holding to the landlord. Compensation is still payable if the tenant quits the holding prior to the termination date even though the 1954 Act ceases to apply to the tenancy on cessation of business use.

However, a tenant must be careful not to quit the holding prematurely particularly as its right to compensation might be subject to an exclusion agreement in the lease. Cessation of business use prior to quitting the holding will cause the tenancy to cease to be one to which the 1954 Act applies such that the anti-avoidance provisions in section 38(2) would not operate to strike down the exclusion agreement. Further, quitting the premises prematurely may disentitle the tenant to double compensation.

Bacchiocchi v Academic Agency Ltd (1998)

The tenant was entitled to compensation even though it vacated the holding 12 days before the termination date. Although there was an exclusion agreement in the lease, that agreement was ineffective because the 1954 Act still applied as at the termination date because cessation of the business prior to quitting was incidental to the business activities of the tenant.

Webb v Sandown Sports Club Ltd (2000)

The tenant was entitled to compensation where it quit the holding and withdrew its application for a new tenancy after the termination date specified in the section 25 notice but prior to the termination date provided for by section 64 of the 1954 Act. It was held that the tenant was entitled to compensation on quitting even though the landlord subsequently forfeited the tenancy at a time when the Act did not apply to it.

10.5 AMOUNT OF COMPENSATION

Section 37(2) of the 1954 Act provides that the tenant will either be entitled to single or double compensation calculated according to the statutory formula. Single compensation is the amount of the rateable value of the holding (as shown on the valuation list in force at the date of the section 25 notice or section 26 request) multiplied by the 'appropriate multiplier'. Double compensation, which is only payable if certain conditions are satisfied, is simply twice the amount of single compensation.

If the relevant valuation date is after 1 April 1990 and any part of the holding constitutes domestic property, reference should be made to the detailed provisions in the Act dealing with calculation of the compensation payable, namely section 31(5A) to 31(5E).

Edicron v William Whiteley (1984)

It was held at first instance that for the purposes of calculating the compensation payable the extent of the holding is to be judged as at the date of service of the section 25 notice. That finding was not challenged on appeal.

Plessy Co plc v Eagle Pension Fund Ltd (1990)

It was held that the rateable value of the holding must be assessed as per the state of the valuation list at the date of valuation so that the tenant could not take advantage of a retrospective amendment to the valuation list.

Landlord and Tenant Act (Appropriate Multiplier) Order 1990 (SI 1990/363)

Under these current regulations (which took effect from 1 April 1990), the 'appropriate multiplier' is one.

10.6 DOUBLE COMPENSATION

If the tenant can satisfy the conditions set out in section 37(3) of the 1954 Act in respect of the whole of the holding, double compensation will be payable. In all other cases, the tenant will only be entitled to single compensation. There are now express provisions which allow for an aggregate sum to be paid where the conditions are satisfied in relation to part of the holding only with double compensation being paid for that part and single compensation being paid in respect of the other part.

Landlord and Tenant Act 1954, section 37(3)

Under this provision the conditions for obtaining double compensation are:

- that during the whole of the 14 years immediately prior to termination of the current tenancy (being the date specified in the section 25 notice or section 26 request), premises being or comprised in the holding have been occupied for the purposes of a business carried on by the occupier or for those and other purposes;
- that if during those 14 years there was a change in the occupier of the premises, the person who was the occupier immediately after the change was the successor to the business carried on by the person who was the occupier immediately before the change.

Landlord and Tenant Act 1954, section 37(3A)

Section 37(3A), which was introduced by the *Regulatory Reform (Business Tenancies) (England and Wales) Order* 2003 ('2003 Order'), makes provision for a differential calculation of compensation where only part of the holding satisfies the conditions in section 37(3) of the 1954 Act. In such a case, the compensation will be the aggregate of the compensation sums calculated separately in respect of each part. So, for example, if the higher rate of compensation could be established in relation to part of the premises, compensation may be calculated separately in relation to that part.

Cramas Properties Ltd v Connaught Fur Trimmings Ltd (1965)

If there is a change in occupation during the 14-year period, in order for double compensation to be payable, the new occupier must be the successor of the actual business belonging to the previous occupier. It is not sufficient that merely the same type of business is carried on.

Bacchiocchi v Academic Agency Ltd (1998)

It was held that cessation of business activities by the tenant shortly before the termination date was incidental to the ordinary course of a business which involved running down a business to quit on the proper date and therefore was not to be discounted for the purposes of deciding whether double compensation was payable. On this basis, periods of fitting out which are also incidental to a business should not be discounted either. In each case, it will be a question of fact and degree whether the cessation of trading is incidental to the business in question.

Sight and Sound Education Ltd v Books Etc Ltd (1999)

The court held that the tenant was not entitled to double compensation because it had quit the premises prior to the termination date specified in the section 25 notice and therefore had not occupied the premises for the purposes of its business during the whole of the 14 years immediately prior to the termination of the current tenancy.

10.7 CONTRACTING OUT OF THE COMPENSATION PROVISIONS

Section 38(2) of the 1954 Act provides that an agreement relating to a tenancy to which the Act applies (whether contained in the tenancy agreement itself or not and whether made before or after the termination of the tenancy) which purports to exclude or reduce the compensation payable under section 37 of the Act will be void to that extent.

However, such an agreement excluding or limiting such compensation will be enforceable in two scenarios (a) and (b), namely:

(a) Where the preconditions to the operation of section 38(2) are not satisfied. The preconditions are that:

- during the whole of the five years immediately prior to the date on which the tenant is to quit the holding, the premises being, or comprised in, the holding have been occupied for the purposes of a business carried on by the occupier or for those and other purposes; and
- if during those five years there was a change in the occupier of the premises, the person who was the occupier immediately after the change was the successor to the business carried on by the person who was the occupier immediately before the change.

(b) Where an agreement as to the amount of any such compensation is made after the right to compensation has accrued.

London Baggage Co (Chancery Cross) Ltd v Railtrack plc (No 2) (2003)

The lease contained a clause excluding compensation where the tenant had been in occupation for less than five years immediately preceding the date the lease determined. The tenant had failed to serve any counter notice (as was required at the time) and so the tenancy came to an end on the date specified in the landlord's section 25 notice. At that time, the tenant had only been in been in occupation for about four years. From the expiry of the lease, the tenant continued in occupation as a tenant at will for a further

20 months before quitting. The tenant's claim to compensation was dismissed on the grounds that the only period of occupation under section 38(2) which counted was occupation of premises under a tenancy protected by the 1954 Act. Since the tenant had only been in occupation of the premises under the protected tenancy for four years, the exclusion clause was operative.

10.8 COMPENSATION FOR MISREPRESENTATION

If the court refuses to order a new tenancy but it is subsequently shown that the court was induced to refuse the grant by misrepresentation or the concealment of material facts, the court may, under section 37A(1) of the 1954 Act, order the landlord to pay the tenant such sum as appears sufficient as compensation for damage or loss sustained by the tenant as a result of the order or refusal.

The reforms affected by the 2003 Order also empower the court to order the landlord to pay compensation to the tenant where the tenant has been induced by reason of any misrepresentation or the concealment of material facts to quit the holding either without making any application or after withdrawing such an application (see section 37A(2)).

These provisions are most likely to be of relevance where the tenant has accepted the landlord's assertion that he intends to redevelop the premises and/or occupy them for his own business purposes but subsequently finds out that the landlord misrepresented his intentions.

Fisher v Taylors Furnishing Stores Ltd (1956)

The tenant will not be entitled to compensation if the landlord has merely subsequently changed its mind in good faith. What is required is a misrepresentation of the landlord's intention as at the time the representation was made.

11
Interim rent

11.1 OLD LAW

The interim rent provisions have been amended by the *Regulatory Reform (Business Tenancies) (England and Wales) Order* 2003 ('2003 Order') which has repealed the old section 24 of the *Landlord and Tenant Act* 1954 ('1954 Act') and inserted new sections 24A to 24D. In essence, the new provisions apply if the relevant section 25 notice was given or section 26 request made on or after 1 June 2004. For interim rent applications arising out of a notice given or request made before that date, reference should be made to the repealed provision which is not dealt with in detail in this book, although many of the old cases remain relevant.

Previously, only a landlord could apply for an interim rent and in circumstances where market rents were falling, a landlord would refrain from seeking an interim rent on the basis that the tenant would have to continue paying the higher rent under the old tenancy until the new tenancy came into effect. This was obviously most unfair to tenants and it was thought right to allow the tenants to apply for an interim rent to prevent this in the future.

It was also the case that the interim rent would run only from the date the application was made or the date specified in the landlord's notice or tenant's request, whichever was the later. The interim rent was valued by reference to the rent under the new tenancy but having regard to the rent payable under the old tenancy and an assumption that the new tenancy would be granted from year to year.

11.2 NEW LAW

11.2.1 Who can make an application?

Landlord and Tenant Act 1954, section 24A(1) and (2)

Under the new section 24A, both the landlord and the tenant now have the right to make an application for the determination of an interim rent unless the other party has already made (and not withdrawn) an application. An interim rent is the rent which the tenant pays while the tenancy is continued under section 24.

11.2.2 Time for application

Landlord and Tenant Act 1954, section 24A(1) and (3)

An application may be made at any time after the landlord has served a section 25 notice or the tenant has made a section 26 request. However, an application will not be entertained if it is made more than six months after the termination of the continuation tenancy.

11.2.3 Date from which interim rent payable ('the appropriate date')

Landlord and Tenant Act 1954, section 24B

The date from which the interim rent is payable is referred to as 'the appropriate date' and differs depending on whether a section 25 notice has been given or a section 26 request made. If the landlord has given notice under section 25 then the 'appropriate date' is the earliest date of termination that could have been specified in his notice. If the tenant has made a section 26 request then the 'appropriate date' is the earliest date which could have been specified in the tenant's request as the date from which the new tenancy is to begin.

11.2.4 Amount of interim rent

The basis of calculating the amount of the interim rent will differ depending on whether a new lease of the whole of the premises has been granted on an unopposed basis or not. It will be important to identify at the outset whether the application falls within sections 24C or 24D of the 1954 Act. An expert will need to be very specific as to the relevant provisions he or she is providing an expert opinion in respect of. Expert evidence may be needed on a variety of issues relevant to interim rent, namely:

(a) to demonstrate, under section 24C(3), that there has been a substantial change in the market or that changes in the terms of the new tenancy have a substantial effect on the rent;
(b) to assist the court in determining the relevant rent under section 24C(4);
(c) to assist the court in determining the interim rent under section 24C(6) and (7); and
(d) to assist the court in determining the interim rent under section 24D.

Any expert must refer to the detailed provisions of the relevant sections prior to preparing his or her report.

Amount where unopposed grant of new tenancy of whole of premises: section 24C

In this case, under section 24C of the 1954 Act, the rent payable under and at the commencement of the new tenancy will also be the interim rent, unless either the landlord or the tenant shows to the satisfaction of the court:

- a substantial change in the market; or
- a change in the terms of the new lease which substantially affects the rent.

Under section 24C(5), if the new rent is not appropriate only because of a substantial change in the market then the interim rent will be the relevant rent, namely the market rent which would payable (under section 34) in respect of the new tenancy if it commenced on the appropriate date.

Under section 24C(6), if the court has to determine the interim rent because it is not satisfied that it is appropriate for the new rent to also be the interim rent because of a change in the terms of the new lease which substantially affects the rent (whether or not there has also been a substantial change in the market), the interim rent is the rent which it is reasonable for the tenant to pay while the relevant tenancy is continued by the Act, having regard to:

- the rent payable under the terms of the continuation tenancy and any subtenancy of part of the property comprised in the continuation tenancy; and
- the rent which would be payable under subsections 34(1) and (2) in respect of a tenancy of the whole of the property comprised in the old tenancy for the same duration as the new tenancy which is actually granted.

Amount in any other case: section 24D

Where section 24C of the 1954 Act does not apply, the interim rent is determined under section 24D. In such cases, the interim rent will be the amount the court considers it reasonable for the tenant to pay while the relevant tenancy continues having regard to:

- the rent payable under the terms of the continuation tenancy and any subtenancy of part of the property comprised in the continuation tenancy;
- the rent which would be payable under subsections 34(1) and (2) in respect of a tenancy from year to year of the whole of the property in the old tenancy.

11.2.5 Grant of an interim rent is discretionary

Although both the landlord and the tenant have the right to apply for a determination of an interim rent, the court is not bound to order an interim rent. Section 24A(1) of the 1954 Act provides that the court *may* order payment of an interim rent. This was also the case under the old law but in most cases the court would determine an interim rent. Especially now that the tenant also has the right to apply for the determination of an interim rent, it is difficult to think of circumstances in which the court would refuse to make such an order.

English Exporters v Eldonwall (1973)

Although the grant of an interim rent is discretionary, in most normal cases the discretion ought to be exercised in favour of determining such a rent. The court is not given a roving commission to consider every fact that might bear on reasonableness but must (under the old provisions) determine what rent it would be reasonable for the tenant to pay according to the market value formula of section 34 but having regard to the rent payable under the existing tenancy. The same principle would apply to the specific requirements under the new provisions.

Bloomfield v Ashwright Ltd (1983)

In this case under the old provisions, Lawton LJ accepted that the court had the discretion to order an interim rent and therefore might refuse to do so but indicated that he found it difficult to imagine circumstances in which it would be unjust to the tenant to order an interim rent.

Charles Follett Ltd v Cabtell Investments Ltd (1987)

It was held, under the old provisions, that the court has no discretion to order the tenant to pay anything other or less than the interim rent as determined and the reasoning would apply equally to the new provisions.

11.2.6 The statutory cushion

In determining the interim rent under sections 24C and 24D, the 1954 Act provides that the court is to have regard to the old rent. In respect of the same wording in the old provisions, it was held that this confers on the court discretion to cushion the market rent. The court has no discretion to cushion the rent if, under section 24C, the interim rent is the same rate as the rent under the new tenancy or is valued under section 24C(5). The application of a cushion to the market rent under sections 24C(6) and 24D is a matter for the court's discretion and not valuation evidence. As a matter of good practice, an expert valuer should make it clear in his or her report that no statutory cushion has been applied and that the expert opinion relates solely to the appropriate market rental valuation carried in accordance with the relevant provisions of sections 24A to 24D. Whilst in one case the court discounted by 50%, in other cases the courts have not applied any cushion. Courts often apply a cushion of about 8% to 15% but this is not a strict rule and the question as to the appropriate cushion is a matter for legal submission in each case.

Charles Follett Ltd v Cabtell Investments Ltd (1987)

Nourse LJ indicated that the purpose of the direction to have regard to the old rent is to cushion the tenant against the shock of the consequences of inflation being visited upon him in full directly after the old lease is determined. In that case, the court discounted the market rent by 50% to cushion the rent.

French v Commercial Union Life Assurance Co plc (1993)

The longer the period of the continuation tenancy, the less the statutory cushion is likely to be.

11.2.7 Hearing of interim rent application

In practice, the court will often hear evidence relating to the interim rent application at the same time as the substantive hearing and it will be necessary to prepare for trial accordingly. There is of course nothing to stop the parties agreeing the interim rent separately from the main action. The valuation evidence will usually be different from that appropriate to the determination of the rent payable under the new tenancy. In particular, the valuation date will differ and, where section 24D of the 1954 Act applies, the hypothetical tenancy in respect of which rent is determined is a tenancy from year to year. The annual rental on a year-to-year tenancy almost always comes out lower than that in respect of the fixed term new tenancy. An expert should deal with the valuation of interim rent in a separate part of his or her report and should refer expressly to the relevant sections of the Act dealing with interim rent.

Arora v Bose (1998)

This was a case under the old provisions but the principle applies equally to the new provisions. The court dismissed an interim rent application where no evidence relating to the application was adduced during the course of the substantive hearing.

Fawke v Viscount Chelsea (1980)

The court has discretion to order a differential market rent which will be appropriate if that is what would have been agreed on the market during the interim period. In this case, a differential rent was ordered to take account of repairs carried out during the interim period which justified a higher rent on completion. In valuing the interim rent, the court should take into account the state of repair of the premises as they actually stood during the interim period.

11.2.8 Change of circumstances

Landlord and Tenant Act 1954, section 24D(3)

Section 24D(3) provides that if the court has made an order for the grant of a new tenancy and has ordered payment of an interim rent in accordance with section 24C of the Act, but either it subsequently revokes the order pursuant to a tenant's request under section 36(2) or the landlord and the tenant agree not to act on the order, the court, on the application of either the landlord or the tenant, shall determine a new interim rent in accordance with section 24D without a further application being made.

12
Finalising the process

Following final hearing, the renewal process will be concluded in one of two ways. Where the landlord successfully opposes the grant of a new tenancy, the effect will be that the current tenancy will determine in accordance with statutory provisions and unless the landlord subsequently allows the tenant to remain in occupation, the tenant will have to vacate the premises. If the grant of a new tenancy is not opposed or the landlord's opposition is unsuccessful, the process will be finalised by the execution of a new lease following the making of an order for a new tenancy (or an agreement to that effect).

12.1 OPPOSITION TO A NEW TENANCY BY A LANDLORD

The landlord may successfully oppose the grant of a new tenancy either by defending the tenant's application for the grant of a new tenancy or in the context of its own application for an order terminating the tenancy without the grant of a new tenancy under section 29(2) of the *Landlord and Tenant Act* 1954 ('1954 Act').

Landlord and Tenant Act 1954, section 31(1)

Section 31(1) provides that if the landlord successfully opposes the grant of a new tenancy on any of the grounds specified in section 30(1) of the Act, the tenant's application for a new tenancy will be dismissed.

Landlord and Tenant Act 1954, section 29(4)

Section 29(4) provides that where the landlord makes an application to the court for an order for the termination of the tenancy without the grant of a new tenancy under section 29(2) and establishes any of the grounds of opposition, the court must make an order for termination of the current tenancy in accordance with section 64 of the Act without the grant of the new tenancy.

12.2 DISMISSAL ON OTHER GROUNDS

The tenant's application for a new tenancy might also be dismissed for other reasons, such as where the court makes an order following failure to comply with a court direction. The application will also be dismissed where the tenancy ceases to be one to which the 1954 Act applies such as where there is a cessation of business user.

Civil Procedure Rules 1998 ('CPR'), Rule 3.4

Rule 3.4 gives the court power to dismiss an application where:

(i)   there are no reasonable grounds for making the application;
(ii)   the application is an abuse of process; or
(iii) there has been a failure to comply with a rule, practice direction or court order.

Landlord and Tenant Act 1954, section 31(2)

In some cases, the court will not grant a new tenancy even where the landlord has not been successful in establishing grounds of opposition.

Under section 31(2), where the landlord has unsuccessfully relied upon one or more of grounds (d) (suitable alternative accommodation), (e) (subletting of part) and (f) (redevelopment) but the court would have been satisfied on one or more of those grounds if the date specified in the section 25 notice or section 26 request had been a date later (but not more than a year later) than that which was in fact specified, the court will not make an order for a new tenancy.

For example, the landlord wishing to redevelop might over optimistically specify an early date in its section 25 notice and push ahead for an expedited hearing opposing on ground (f). It might not then be able to show the necessary settled intention to reconstruct a substantial part of the premises as at that termination date because its plans could not at that time be implemented (such as where a planning application is still likely to be pending). However, the court might be satisfied that the landlord would be in a position to do the works at a later date within a year.

In such cases, the court will make a declaration to that effect specifying the alternative date on which the grounds would have been satisfied. The tenant then has 14 days in which to make an application for an order substituting the alternative date for the date actually specified in the notice or request. On the making of such an order, the tenancy will continue until the later termination date. If the tenant does not make such an application, the tenancy will determine in the usual course of events three months and two weeks thereafter pursuant to section 64 of the 1954 Act.

Accountancy Personnel Ltd v Worshipful Company of Salters (1972)

The landlord relied on ground (f). The judge held on the balance of probabilities that the landlord would not obtain the necessary planning permission until six months after the termination date such that ground (f) was not made out. However the judge made a declaration under section 32(2). On appeal it transpired that the planning permission would be delayed further and the Court of Appeal substituted an even later date (but not one that was more than a year from the original termination date).

12.3 TERMINATION OF THE TENANCY

The effect of both a dismissal of the tenant's application and the making of an order terminating the current tenancy without the grant of a new tenancy on the landlord's application is that the current tenancy will determine in accordance with section 64 of the 1954 Act. However, where the application is dismissed under section 31(2) and the tenant makes an application for the substitution of the 'alternative date' in the section 25 notice or section 26 request, the tenancy will not determine until that later date. Note that where the tenant quits prior to the contractual term date, the tenancy will end on that contractual term date even if the tenant has made an application for a new tenancy prior to that date.

Landlord and Tenant Act 1954, section 64

The effect of section 64 is that on dismissal or the making of an order terminating the tenancy, the continuation tenancy continues thereafter for a period of three months beginning with the date on which the application is finally disposed of unless the section 25 notice or section 26 request specified a later date of termination (which is rarely the case). The reference to the date on which the application is finally disposed of allows time for a possible appeal. This means in practice in respect of an order that is not actually appealed that the tenancy will expire in the usual course of events three months and two weeks after the date of the order. Where an appeal is made, the tenancy will be continued until three months after dismissal of the final appeal.

Single Horse Properties Ltd v Surrey County Council (2002)

Where a landlord had served a notice under section 25 and the tenant had made an application for a new tenancy but had then quit the premises prior to the contractual term date, the tenancy was not continued under section 24(1) and the section 25 notice was of no effect to terminate the tenancy and therefore section 64(1)(c) was not engaged. The tenant was therefore not liable for rent between the contractual term date and the date being three months and two weeks after the claim for a new tenancy was subsequently struck out (namely the date unsuccessfully contended for by the landlords as being the date of termination under section 64).

12.4 YIELDING UP

The tenant usually has a period of just over three months following the final disposal of the application in which to vacate the premises. If the tenant fails to vacate within this period, possession proceedings could be commenced on the expiry of the period as the tenant would remain in occupation thereafter as a trespasser.

On the tenant yielding up the premises it would be usual for the landlord to thereafter prepare a schedule of terminal dilapidations depending on the condition of the premises and the repairing obligations in the lease.

Civil Procedure Rules 1998, Part 55

Part 55 sets out the procedure for making an application to the County Court for a possession order including a possession order against a former tenant holding over without consent on the expiry of the tenancy. Note that such claims against former tenants are not 'trespasser proceedings' for the purposes of Part 55.

12.5 EXECUTION OF THE NEW LEASE

Under section 36(1) of the 1954 Act, if the court makes an order for a new tenancy either on the tenant's application or on the failure of the landlord in its own application for termination of the tenancy to establish grounds of opposition then (unless that order is revoked or the parties agree not to act on it) the landlord is bound to execute and the tenant is bound to accept a lease on the terms agreed or determined by the court. The landlord can require the tenant to execute a counterpart lease. Pursuant to section 36(4) a lease granted pursuant to the Act is treated as having been authorised so far as any mortgagee is concerned.

Landlord and Tenant Act 1954, section 29(1)

Section 29(1) provides that the court shall make an order for the grant of a new tenancy (and for the termination of the current tenancy immediately before the commencement of the new tenancy) on the tenant's application under section 24(1) if the landlord fails to make out grounds of opposition.

Landlord and Tenant Act 1954, section 29(4)

Section 29(4) provides that where the landlord's application under section 29(2) for the termination of the current tenancy is unsuccessful due to the landlord failing to establish to the court's satisfaction any of the grounds on which he is entitled to make such an application under section 30, the court shall make an order for the grant of a new tenancy and accordingly for the termination of the current tenancy immediately before the commencement of the new tenancy.

12.6 TENANCY COMMENCEMENT DATE

The court is given no discretion as to the commencement date of the new tenancy. Section 33 of the 1954 Act provides that the new tenancy shall begin on the coming to an end of the current tenancy.

Where an application has been made, in most cases, the existing tenancy will not terminate (in accordance with section 64) until three months and two weeks after the date of the order. The order for a new tenancy is for a new tenancy commencing on the expiry of the current tenancy.

Michael Chipperfield v Shell UK Ltd (1980)

The Court of Appeal observed that in making the order for a new tenancy the date on which the tenancy was to expire should be expressly stated, given the difficulty in knowing exactly when the tenancy was to commence.

12.7 EFFECT OF NEW TENANCY ON REVERSIONARY INTERESTS

There are detailed provisions in the 1954 Act dealing with the effect of the grant of a new tenancy on reversionary titles. For example, if the tenancy which is renewed is one of a chain of tenancies, the practical effect of a statutory renewal may be to extend the term beyond the term date of a superior tenancy. A detailed examination of these provisions is beyond the scope of this work but the relevant provisions are set out in section 65 and the Schedule 6 to which further reference should be made if necessary.

12.8 FAILURE TO EXECUTE LEASE

It is unclear exactly how the parties might enforce such an order in default but it is thought that an application to the court should be made either for specific performance and/or for execution of the lease by a court officer. Since the existing tenancy does not terminate until three months after the order, it is thought that an application for compliance with an order should not be made before that time.

Greaves Organisation v Stanhope Gate Property Co (1973)

The effect of an order for the grant of a new tenancy is that the tenant has an equitable lease as the position is analogous to the situation where an agreement for lease has been entered into.

Pulleng v Curran (1980)

An order under section 29 of the 1954 Act is to be regarded as an agreement for lease on the terms of the order.

12.9 AGREEMENT NOT TO ACT ON THE ORDER

Following the making of an order for a new tenancy, the landlord and tenant may agree not to act upon it.

Landlord and Tenant Act 1954, section 69(2)

Any such agreement not to proceed must be in writing.

Law of Property (Miscellaneous Provisions) Act 1989, section 2

As the court order creates an equitable lease, any agreement between the parties not to proceed would amount to an agreement to surrender which must be in writing containing all the terms of the agreement and signed by or on behalf of all parties to be enforceable under section 2.

12.10 APPLICATION BY TENANT FOR REVOCATION OF THE ORDER

The tenant is given 14 days to consider whether he is willing to take on the burden of the new tenancy as ordered by the court. The court has no discretion to refuse an application for revocation made by the tenant. The court does have discretion to revoke or vary any order for costs that was made, or award costs if no costs order was made.

Landlord and Tenant Act 1954, section 36(2)

Section 36(2) provides that the tenant may apply for the revocation of the order within 14 days of the order being made.

Index

Index

The Case in Point series

The *Case in Point* series is an exiting new set of concise practical guides to legal issues in land, property and construction. Written for the property professional, they get straight to the key issues in a refreshingly jargon-free style.

Areas covered:

Negligence in Valuation and Surveys
Stock code: 6388
Published: December 2002

Party Walls
Stock code: 7269
Published: May 2004

Service Charges
Stock code: 7272
Published: June 2004

Estate Agency
Stock code: 7472
Published: July 2004

Rent Review
Stock code: 8531
Published: May 2005

Publishing soon:
Expert Witness
VAT in Property and Construction

If you would like to be kept informed when new *Case in Point* titles are published, please e-mail **rbmarketing@rics.org.uk**

How to order:

All RICS Books titles can be ordered direct by:

☎ Telephoning 0870 333 1600 (Option 3)
🖱 Online at www.ricsbooks.com
📠 E-mail mailorder@rics.org.uk